Dedicated to my loved ones.

Thank you for
your prayers,
your thoughts,
and
your support:
They fueled the fire
of my recovery.

You're never really alone.

TABLE OF CONTENTS

Chapter	Page

Diana, Michael, Laurén, Bryan, me

Introduction

In August of two-thousand and five, I was diagnosed with appendix cancer. This is a rare (one in a quarter million) form of metastatic carcinoma that, according to many sources, has less than a twenty percent survival rate. Needless to say, at the young age of fifty-five, with a lovely wife, three incredible children, a dental practice at the top of its game, and everything to live for, this news was devastating. The gamut of emotions I felt was overwhelming. Fortunately, within a reasonable time, I put my faith in God. Not surprisingly, He led me to the right people and places, and provided me with the outpouring of love and support from friends and family that enabled me to jump the hurdles of this trial.

During my conversations with God after my surgery, I felt that I was supposed to share my experiences where He has been instrumental in my life. I believe that He wanted me to do this so that others would be more accepting that He is always there, and sometimes we need to do is look a little harder to see Him as part of our daily lives. There is a metaphor of a man who while walking on the beach of life sees God's footsteps along side him at all times except during the man's hardships. The man confronts God and asks why He abandoned him at those times when He was needed the most. "There was only one set of footprints in the sand and You were not beside me," the man said. God responded to the man, "There was only one set of footprints in the sand, and they were mine. I was carrying you, my son."

That story is what this book is all about. There have been so many times in my life where I was carried and nestled in the palm of God. The most recent and most frightening was my battle with cancer. Now, on the other side of the fight, I have no doubt that I am happy and healthy today because of the skill of my doctors and my faith in God. This book does not choose a specific organized religious path: It paints a broader picture of a man's relationship with God, and more specifically, shares with you stories of His presence in this **survivors** life.

Third hole at Orange Hills Golf Club

Al Got a Hole in One

A hole-in-one is a rarity. Most golfers will play their entire lives and never get one. It is the mini-miracle of the sports world. Either the golfer who gets the hole in one is incredibly talented (which most golfers are not), or as I have always believed, there is a powerful force called God that picks up your ball, carries it a hundred-plus yards and drops it in the hole. You just happen to be lucky enough to be there when it happens.

On Friday, August nineteenth, 2005, at seven o'clock in the morning, my golfing partner of five years got a hole in one on the third hole at Orange Hills Golf Course. That divine force was with Al and me that morning. God has been with me all of my life; He just happened to make His presence more noticeable when he picked up Al's golf ball and placed it in the hole.

His timing, as usual, was impeccable: God's, not Al's. That Friday was one of those marked days when the decisions I would make would determine the future of my life.

Several weeks prior to this round of golf I had undergone hernia surgery, and through biopsies, the surgeon had detected a metastatic cancerous growth within my abdomen. He sent me for a colonoscopy and then a CT scan. The official diagnosis was Metastatic Adenocarcenoma Myxoma Peritonea stemming from the appendix. When I Googled this disease (the way most of us look for vital information nowadays), the prognosis was bleak. Most sites quoted survival rates in the twenty percent range.

As I began the round of golf that Friday, my mind would not

budge from the call I would make to the surgeon to schedule surgery for the following week. I'd made up my stubborn mind that I would have the local surgeon who had performed the hernia operation operate a second time. My wife, Diana, was adamant that I call Sloan Kettering Cancer Center in New York for a second opinion. In my frustration, I had rebuffed her and ignorantly decided to go ahead with the local doctor for the sake of convenience.

By the third hole during that Friday's golf round, my mind was far from the game. Al on the other hand had made some lucky shots and was verbally jabbing me as usual. He was unaware of the turmoil in my head, as he stepped up to the third tee and confidently stated that he was going to get a hole in one. He took his usual mechanical swing, and the ball flew a hundred and thirty-eight yards, bounced on the green, and slowly rolled into the hole.

Al was doubtful that his ball actually went into the hole, and believed that it had rolled past. "I saw it go in," I said with confidence. Considering my state of mind at the time, I instantly saw a connection between his hole in one and the presence of God on the golf course. This is where my leap of faith occurs. His hole in one could have been seen as just that: a hole in one. I, on the other hand, read into this occurrence a spiritual communication: a sign that God was communicating with me and that I needed to listen closely in order to hear what He was trying to tell me. My senses were heightened for the rest of the day.

"Please call Sloan Kettering Hospital," Diana softly said as soon as I walked through the front door that afternoon after my round of golf. The tone of her voice was filled with concern, power, and love. I heard more than her words; I heard God talking to me. Without hesitating, I walked over to the phone and dialed Sloan Kettering Hospital. Al's hole in one had heightened my receptiveness to signals. As odd as this may sound, I followed Diana's request to call Sloan Kettering simply because Al got a hole in one.

The Sloan people were kind and accommodating. After finding the correct department, I was connected to a lady who was totally familiar with my form of cancer. She informed me that appendix cancer was so rare that they had seen less than sixty cases at Sloan Kettering Hospital. She advised me that a physician in Washington, D.C. was more familiar with this cancer, but a surgeon in New Haven, Connecticut was also well known for his expertise. She also clearly stated that the surgical procedure was a significant component of the cure, and that choosing the right physician was critical. The difference between someone who had seen this disease and someone who had not could be the difference between life and death.

I took her advice seriously and after our forty-five minute conversation, I called Dr. Ron Salem at Yale New Haven Hospital in Connecticut, about twenty minutes from my home. It was just before two o'clock on that Friday afternoon when I left a message with his answering service. They informed me that he was in surgery, and he would call me back when his procedure was finished. Moments later, Dr. Salem returned my call, and with a smooth, clear confident voice offered to see me for a consultation any time within the next hour. He would need my pathology report, CT scan, and the colonoscopy CD in order to make our consultation worthwhile. He doubted that an hour was ample time for me to get all the information and make the drive to his office, but I informed him that my golf partner had gotten a hole in one that morning, and I would be there with everything that he needed before three o'clock. I am sure that he did not quite understand the hole in one part of our conversation, but I knew that I would make it to his office in the allotted time with all of the data that he needed.

My next call was to Paul, a friend who is connected with Milford Hospital where I had my medical records. Without any hesitation, he agreed that Dr. Salem was one of the finest abdominal surgeons and further informed me that he would have copies of all of the necessary information waiting for me in ten minutes at Milford Hospitals admissions desk. Diana and I jumped in the car, and found Paul waiting in the parking lot of the hospital with my folder in hand. He smiled as Diana and I thanked him profusely. He wished me luck and shooed us on our way.

Traffic on Interstate 95 North to New Haven at two-thirty on Friday afternoon was, as usual, backed up for miles. Using back roads and God's help with the red lights, we made it to Dr. Salem's office five minutes before three. His staff was expecting me and ushered me in after relieving me of my records. His nurse took my vitals within minutes, and Dr. Salem came into the room about ten minutes later after having read the medical data.

Dr. Salem was just as I pictured: a mild-mannered, confident, and sensitive man. He stood nearly six feet tall with dark hair and calming brown eyes. His moderate frame housed a healing giant. We talked while he examined me, for about forty-five minutes, and then he concurred with the diagnosis of appendix cancer.

"It is a rare form of cancer and there is not enough data to prove which treatment modality works best," he said. This was not comforting, but his honesty was refreshing. He still seemed confident that he could treat me successfully.

At the end of the appointment, I was positive that this was the man I wanted to handle my medical condition. The surgeon who had performed my hernia operation is a fine practitioner, but he had never treated this specific cancer. I believed that I had been directed here by God, and I felt good about my decision. Before leaving Dr. Salem's office, I requested a specific surgical date two weeks away. This would allow me to bring my son, Michael, to his first year of college, and leave several days between the operation and my daughter Laurén's departure for a year in Ecuador. Laurén could see me off the operating table and be able to go with a clearer conscience for her volunteer commitment. She would have canceled her trip had things not gone right.

Dr. Salem smiled and then informed me that the scheduling was out of his bounds. The hospital had control of the timing specifics.

"That's all right," I said, "Al got a hole in one today: God is on my side." He smiled and acknowledged that maybe I would get lucky and get the date that would fit my schedule.

As he turned towards the door, I asked him if I was his last patient because of the length of time we had spent chatting. "You are my only patient. My surgery finished early, and when I got your call, I was ready to leave. I figured that if you could get here within an hour, I would finish up some paperwork and wait for you. Your timing was rather fortuitous."

"Al got a Hole in One today," I repeated, inferring The Higher Power's participation in my day.

"So I have heard," Dr. Salem responded with a smile.

Two weeks later (on the day that I had requested), I was wheeled into the operating room where I spent the next eleven hours. Dr. Salem cleaned, re-cleaned, and cleaned again my abdomen to be sure that he had removed all of the cancerous cells that he could possibly remove. He also removed half of my colon, my appendix, part of my spleen, and the entire lining of my peritoneal cavity that was laced with cancerous cells. Three tubes were placed in my abdomen for drainage; a nasopharyngeal tube was placed in my nose that extended to my stomach so that I would not get any fluids in my gut; a catheter was placed into my urethra so my urine would go directly into a bottle; and two intravenous lines were left in my arm and forehand for medicines to enter and blood to exit my body. This gloomy package was tied up with about fifty stitches from my pubic area to my chest. What a sight I was.

The concurrent cure was chemotherapy from an equally caring group recommended by Dr. Salem. He was hopeful that Oncologist Dr. Jill Lacy would be able to accommodate me into her schedule. Sure enough, she had an opening, and thus my *luck* in finding the right people continued.

Six courses of hospitalized chemotherapy for three days each started the treatments, interlaced with twelve three-day sessions of intravenous chemotherapy to kill the cancer cells from another angle. The nursing staff in the chemotherapy lounge (especially Leah with her bright smile) was as compassionate as Dr. Lacy and her assistant, Carol, and made this part of the adventure less traumatic.

Lessons

When out-of-the-ordinary things happen like a Hole in One, look around and see what messages you receive. Great messages are not always preceded by spectacular events, but if something spectacular occurs, you should tune in your senses to look for signs and direction.

On a daily basis you can look for spiritual directional signs. They seem to flow easier to you if you consciously accept that they exist and that they are real.

Do not be afraid to look for them. Signs are all good: They are sent to you to help you through this confusing world.

Your interpretation of the signs may not always be correct. This is a crucial part of believing in signs. Be sure that you do not overcomplicate the message with any negativity.

If you believe that the message you interpreted was a bad omen, then look for another message that will show you how to counter the first. There are always alternatives, and different messages will lead you down different paths. Even a negative message will have some positive twist for you or someone connected to you. Use the positive to make yourself accept what might not be appealing to you. Life is not always full of rose petals; the thorns that are part of the rose are just as important to the life of the rose as the sweet smell of its blossom.

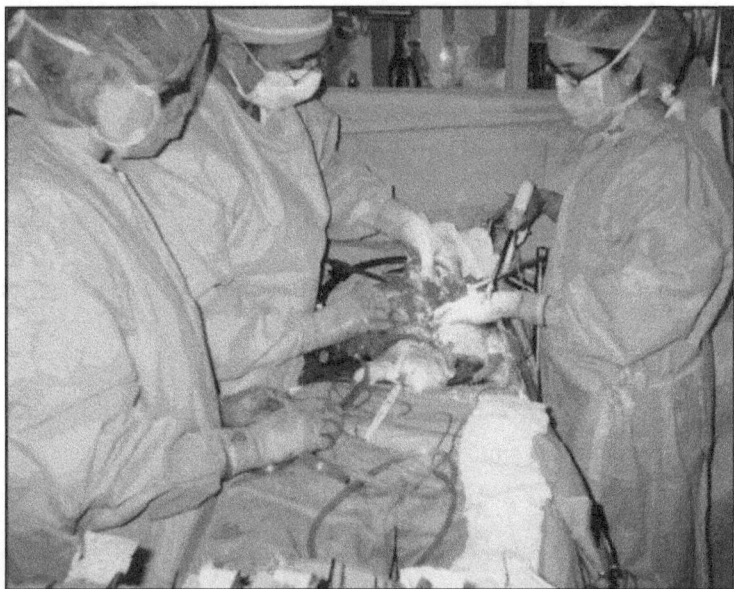

My Surgery

Angels

As far back as I can remember I have believed that the choices one makes and the paths that one takes are somewhat under the guidance of an angel or some spiritual being that wants to assist you. If you are receptive and allow the angel to guide you, life's journey can be much smoother. That's not to say that you don't have a choice in your decisions, but a lot of choices are difficult and often you are unsure of what you should choose: profession, marriage, the merits of a vacation or home purchase, etc. The decisions are fully yours, but if you ask for assistance and look for a spiritual guide, they will appear.

I had been sharing that philosophy with Laurén, my twenty-two year old daughter, after her graduation from Georgetown University. She majored in English and was unsure of what she should do with her life. Certainly she could become anything she wanted: a lawyer, a teacher, a business person, a graduate student, a counselor…, but in her own mind and heart she had not yet found her calling. She's a wonderful soul and an incredibly intelligent person. We had discussed her options, and with my best fatherly advice, I was comfortable in telling her that whatever she chose as her direction, she should look for some spiritual guidance. She saw this as a cop-out because I did not give her definitive answers to her question. Still unsure, she was not enthusiastic or confident with any options that lay before her.

With considerable personal turmoil, she had found the WorldTeach program, sponsored by Harvard University's Center for International Development. This was an accepted, fully-accredited endeavor where she would be living with a family in Ecuador and teaching the English language to adults in her town. She would commit a year of her life to the worthwhile goal of helping others communicate more globally, thereby helping their economic status and their lives in general. It also gave her the chance to travel and improve her language skills.

On the day of my cancer surgery, two days before she was supposed to go to Ecuador, Laurén confronted her decision to commit to the program. Uncertainty was the mood of the moment as it related to her upcoming departure. She was ready to call the program director and withdraw from the list of volunteers.

We received a call at nine that morning asking us to be in the operating room by ten o'clock instead of the scheduled twelve o'clock for the surgery. Anxious to get it under way, I hurried my daughter and my wife into the car. We were in New Haven by nine-thirty and shortly thereafter I kissed Laurén and Diana goodbye before being soldiered into the operating room. My girls took their battle positions in the waiting room where they would be stationed for the next eleven hours.

The empty seats in the waiting room were scattered, and Laurén had to sit apart from her mom. The separation was not too difficult as they both had projects to work on: Diana handling some necessary paperwork and Laurén finishing some editing on a book that I had written.

There Laurén sat, worrying about her father, doing a project that only half-heartedly interested her, while questioning her decision to leave her country and the people she loved for an entire year. Was it what she should be doing? Should she not go? Should she stay here with her father? Should she stay here and get a job?

In a hospital waiting room people tend to be self- insulated and do not necessarily communicate with those nearby. Laurén was listening to her headphones, staring at her computer screen, and only barely noticed a teen wearing army fatigues seated nearby. An elderly man sitting next to her asked the boy, "Are you a Marine?" The teen in the fatigues replied in a subdued manner, "No, they are just clothes." Laurén heard the word "Marine" and took her headphones out of her ears. Her grandfather (Diana's dad) had been a proud Marine and had served during World War II, and the Korean Conflict. Laurén looked at the man sitting next to her and asked, "Are **you** a Marine?"

He responded warmly, "Yes I am." This made her feel somewhat comforted in the fact that maybe her grandfather's spirit was in the waiting room with her now.

Slowly a conversation unfolded. They talked about who they were waiting for. "I'm waiting for my father," Laurén stated.

"I'm waiting for my wife." the man replied.

"Your grandfather was a Marine?" he questioned.

"Yes."

Shortly the conversation turned towards her and Ecuador. "I was stationed in Ecuador", he said. "My wife is Ecuadorian."

"Really!" she said, astonished by the coincidence.

He proceeded to tell her how he had been instrumental in helping local Ecuadorian businessmen form a corporation to make rugs while he was stationed there.

Laurén asked if it was Otovallan rugs, and the man said, "Yes." She had just been reading about these world famous rugs.

"We helped raise six-hundred dollars so we could get a loom," he said. "That was the beginning of their industry."

"What a wonderful thing," she responded.

"You're going there for a year?" he asked.

"Yes, with WorldTeach."

"And is that what you want to do with your life?"

"Well I took the LSAT, but I was a couple of points short to enter the law school I wanted."

"Which law school do you want to go to?"

"NYU or Columbia, maybe," she responded. They talked some more and he proceeded to tell her that he was a lawyer, and that his friend was a professor at NYU School of Law. He assured her that with her participation in this program and her excellent grades, if she wanted to get into law school when she returned from Ecuador, acceptance should not be a problem at all.

He proceeded to tell her that one of his best friends was a lawyer in Quito, Ecuador, and that if she needed anything she would have a friend in Quito. The name of the man next to her was Herman (my dad's first name), and he had law offices in New York and New Haven, and that he would assist her in any way he could. The uplifting feeling and power and security that Laurén felt in meeting this man was amazing.

His wife's surgery was complete, and he left the waiting room at twelve o'clock, which was the time that we were originally supposed to arrive. Had we not come down early, she never would have met this *angel* who made her feel so comfortable in her decision to go to Ecuador and confident that everything would be all right with me.

As this man left the room, Laurén went over to my wife with a beaming smile. She quelled my wife's fears and said that the gentleman she had been talking to for an hour was meant to be there.

She smiled and said, "Mom, Dad's going to be all right, and I believe I am doing the right thing by going to Ecuador." It was as if a weight had been lifted off her shoulders.

It may have been a coincidence that we got to the hospital two hours early; that there was a seat next to this unique individual; and that he was a Marine named Herman who had been stationed in Ecuador, with connections to law schools in New York and also in Quito. Laurén believed, and I agree with her, that it was not a coincidence, but a God-incidence. I am so happy that my daughter's eyes were open enough to allow a guide to help her, and now when I talk to her on her Ecuadorian adventure, she is confident with her path and happy in her life. In her future she will confront other issues and choices, and I hope she will be inclined to look for another guide who will help her choose wisely.

Lessons

Angels do not have to have wings. They can be ordinary people who happen to be in your path and happen to share something with you at some particular time in your life.

You can be someone's angel, and make their burden lighter. You may not even know the effect you have on another's life.

When you communicate with someone, it is easy to impart positive comments, and that's what you should do.

Don't be afraid to communicate with strangers in a safe environment. They may have something valuable to share with you. Then again, you may have something valuable to share with them.

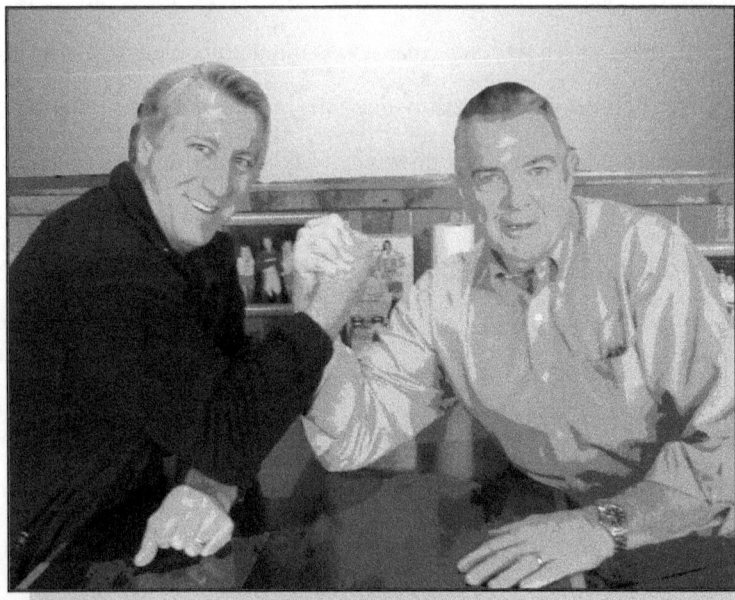

Ken and I meet every month and we are committed to "survive"

Ken: my roommate

The last thing I wanted was a roommate. I wanted a private room with my own space where I could recover. The surgery had gone well according to the surgeon, even though it took a total of eleven hours. The following day spent in the intensive care ward was like a foggy vision filled with pain and the restless passing of time. Diana, Laurén, and many of my friends were with me that day, even though I cannot tell you what transpired. All I know is that I wanted to stay where I was in order to lessen my agony. The people in charge of my medical recovery saw things differently. The intensive care room was no longer to be my domicile with its privacy and constant nursing care.

"Does he really have to leave this room?" Diana protested.

"Yes. He is out of danger, and will be switched to the recovery floor where he will get excellent care; this room is for people that are closer to immediate danger than he is now," the nurse explained.

This good news that my immediate danger had passed was couched in the disappointing information that I would be moving from what I guess was a nice room to one with comparatively less constant care. We took the transfer orders in stride and packed up my personal belongings and flowers that friends had sent. Along with the floral bouquets were a dozen roses that I remember giving away as I traveled through the halls of the hospital on my rolling bed bedecked with tubes and bottles.

Anyone that I passed received a rose: patients, nurses, and

visitors alike. All of the gifted flowers were accepted with smiles and thank you's which, in return, somewhat eased the pain that pervaded my body. When I reached my final destination on the seventh floor of Yale New Haven Hospital, I had one rose left. I gave the final rose to Ken, who would be my roommate for the next forty-eight hours. As I was wheeled through his door, this last rose hid my discontent with having to share a room. He responded by asking, "Does this mean we have to take warm showers together?" somewhat humorously. His comment was lost in my desire to just shut my eyes and fade into a comatose sleep.

He had his own medical story and was confronting his own life and death issues. His surgery was almost as extensive as mine, dealing with a stage-nine, Gleason-scale prostate cancer. His wife and some other people were pretty well settled into his half of this four-hundred-square-foot typical semiprivate recovery room.

"Are there any private rooms?" I heard Diana ask the nurse as we crossed the threshold.

"No." The nurse's response echoed in my throbbing head.

"Are you sure?" Diana asked again somewhat demandingly.

"I'm sorry. All of the private rooms are taken. As soon as one opens up, we'll try to accommodate you," the diplomatic nurse responded, thereby ending the conversation.

In my state, I saw only the suspended white muslin sheet that surrounded my hundred square feet of personal space. The private room would have been nice, but now it seemed that I would be sharing my agony with some stranger and his cadre of guests. He was probably feeling the same way about my invading what had been his private locale.

After settling in for about two hours with nurses poking and prodding me, I said my final goodbye's to Laurén who was leaving for Ecuador the next morning. It was ten o'clock and I was barely awake when Diana kissed me goodbye. My roommate seemed a hundred miles away and my normal gregariousness had evaporated to the point where I had little intention of ever communicating with him.

By two o'clock in the morning, I still had not found any position that did not shoot pain through my mutilated body, and sounds of agony escaped with every attempt to settle down.

"Is my television bothering you?", a voice asked from the dimly-lit other side of the room.

I chuckled in my mind. I couldn't see anything past my suspended sheet; I couldn't hear anything other than my own groans; and I certainly could not be bothered by a television playing so low that even my roommate could barely hear it.

"Nah, I don't think anything could bother me at this point," I said.

I was wrong. A moment later, a nurse sauntered in to take my blood pressure, oxygen levels, temperature, and some blood. Out of curiosity, I asked her what my results were, and her response revealed relatively good vital signs. Then she went to the other man, whose name was Ken, and graced him with the same treatment. He asked the same questions I had, and got similar answers, except that my oxygen level was higher and better. After the nurse left, through my pain, I jokingly said

"I beat you on the oxygen test."

"Yeah, but your pressure was not as good as mine," he correctly stated with a laugh.

That was the beginning of my recovery and Ken's as well. The cosmic force that put us in the same room must have laughed at our relationship from that moment on. There was no malady strong enough to deny our similarly competitive, adventurous, outgoing, and positive personalities. Here we were at the bottom of our games, ludicrously competing over our physical status.

We compared numbers of stitches, types of surgeries, holes in our bodies, quantity of tubes, pain levels, urine outputs, and other such data. When the nurse returned two hours later, she did not seem to understand the importance of who would go first, or why I offered to tip her if she would improve my score. The game was on, and we both knew that we were competing to help the other work through his pain; it was a game we both needed.

Our visitors started coming early the following morning, and surprisingly to them, Ken and I would compare our vitals every few hours when the nurses visited. Our nurses, by this time, knew about the odd couple at the end of the hall and played along by keeping score. The day passed quickly and when everyone left, Ken and I started where we had left off the night before. We compared stories and adventures. Ken's story of his friend "losing a finger on a bear hunting trip and needing to be airlifted out of the backwoods of Canada while Ken stayed and fished" took the blue ribbon in our "can you top this" contest. We compared families, ages, jobs, and future aspirations. Staying cancer-free and getting back to our normal peak levels soon became our agreed upon focus.

"Get up, Rob," Ken said as he slowly raised himself from his bed, leaning on his metal rolling pole that suspended his dripping liquids.

"I can't get up," I said, knowing that the pain would be too much to handle.

"Pain is weakness leaving the body. What doesn't kill you makes you stronger," he responded.

The nurse that was overseeing this latest level of competition agreed with the need to start moving and that we should at least try to get out of bed.

Minutes later, there were Ken and I racing like snails down the hallway, barely moving our feet, poles in hand, johnny coats wide open in the back. We must have gone about ten feet out of our room before we decided to call it a tie and return to our beds, simultaneously pushing the button on our poles that released morphine directly into our painfully screaming bodies.

When Ken left the next day to go home and recover, I cried.

I was moved into a private room, and Diana stayed with me nightly for the next six days until I was released. Diana is a pretty excellent roommate, but only Ken could have provided me with what I needed those first two nights.

Now Ken and I meet once a month for lunch. We compete playing liar's poker, and I have beaten him the last three times, but who's counting?

Lessons

As strong and as capable as you might think you are, there are times when another person is required to help get you out of the mud. In turn, you may also be helping him.

It will not always be your family or friends who will help you get over the hurdles that block your path.

There is always someone in worse shape than you are, even when you are as low as you think you can possibly go.

You never know what a communication will bring. It is relatively easy to listen, respond, and converse with someone. A simple "hello" can start the foundation of an incredible relationship.

We are not meant to be isolated individuals with barriers between us. The more people we come into contact with, the better our chances of living life's adventure to the fullest will be. We will also be adding to someone else's journey. This is what happened between Ken and me.

How many people can you make smile today?

Ultimate Pain

Five days after the operation, I was lucid enough to really feel the pain of my life. I had three intravenous lines: one in the back of each wrist and one in my right inner arm. I also had three gastric drains from my stomach, forty-nine stitches up my midsection, a catheter in my urethra: and a nurse had just removed the nasal gastric tube ran from my nose to my stomach. Fortunately, the morphine drip was still working and tempered the physical pain whenever I pressed my "magic button." At this midday moment, Diana was positioned to my right, and longtime friends, Sue and Joe, were on my left. I have known Sue since I started my practice twenty-eight years ago, and she is still part of my office staff. Many times throughout our friendship, I have been by her side to lend a shoulder or an ear. I was glad to have her at my bedside at that moment.

I squeezed Sue's right hand with my left, gleaning whatever energy and power I could. The mental and physical anguish had drained my last remnants of self-control and machismo. My right hand clutched my cell phone, which was another important factor in my connection to friends and family. The little silver Verizon communicator was a source of immeasurable comfort for me.

My daughter had gone to Ecuador two days after my operation. I was proud of her and thankful that she had decided to go. She left with the understanding that I wanted her to go, and that she had already added what value I needed from her with her comfort, her warmth, and her strong energy. She had landed in Ecuador, was establishing herself, and had already called once.

On this particular Sunday, she called a second time. It was an inopportune time, in my weaked state, to say the least. I flipped the phone open with my right hand and slowly, making sure I did not bend the tube in my right forearm, lifted my hand and placed the cell phone to my ear, still holding Susan's hand with my left. Laurén's voice was full of love, warmth, and a hint of happiness.

"Daddy, how are you?"

"I'm good, sweetheart. I'm good," I responded with every bit of energy I could muster. "How are you, honey?"

"I'm fine," she responded.

"Tell me about you. You talk. I can't talk that much. My throat is sore," I said, suppressing my agony.

Then she began: "Daddy, I am so happy. I love you so much, and miss you. Thank you so much for telling me that I had to go. I already talked to Mom and she said the doctors feel good about you. I am in the right place and doing the right thing. It's amazing, it's absolutely amazing...."

At this point Diana was close to my right side and I reached the phone out and gave it to her. She knew exactly what was happening, and she said to Laurén, "Sweetie, I will keep the phone near Daddy's ear," and she moved it away so that no one could hear the agony that escaped from between my clenched teeth. The suppressed howl of anguish exited my body as a deep, barely-audible moan surrounded by heavy breathing. I couldn't even look at Sue, but I continued to clench her hand. My stomach churned, my arms burned, and my innards boiled over in physical pain as they combined with the intense love and warmth of hearing my daughter's voice filled with happiness.

Laurén knew in her heart and soul that I was going to be okay. Her excited voice sent me to a place where my intense physical pain met my emotional euphoria at a height and depth that I could never have imagined. It was as if a ninety-mile-an-hour freight train decided to turn on a dime, and go the other way.

The conversation ended and I managed to muster a "Goodbye Laurén, I love you," then I hung up the phone and sobbed uncontrollably. Sue, Joe, and Diana could barely understand me between my sobs and tears. My emotions had lost their sense of restraint. Pain and happiness were no longer mutually-exclusive opposite categories. They had been momentarily merged and were one in the same. Pain and pleasure had been shaken so profoundly that the oil and water of feelings were now one substance. The tears flowed and my body heaved in joy and pain simultaneously.

My friends and wife assured me that this was not weakness, and that it was a beautiful moment to have shared. They respected my pain, and they loved me even more for what they had witnessed: tears of love piercing through physical suffering.

Lessons

Someone once equated pain and pleasure with the head and tail of a coin. You couldn't understand pleasure (the head of a coin), unless you knew pain (the tail of a coin). At that moment on that Sunday, I knew exactly what the middle of the coin felt like. The depth of my pain met the height of my pleasure at the center of my penny. At the apex of both sensations, for me, there was an undefined sensation that I will never forget.

Labeling one sensation painful and another sensation pleasurable does not mean that either is more important in our lives. They are both meaningful, even though we would all choose pleasure over pain. From here on forward, it is my choice to believe that at the other end of anything painful there will be an equal and opposite pleasurable component. There is a balance between pain and pleasure. I have seen the center of the extremes.

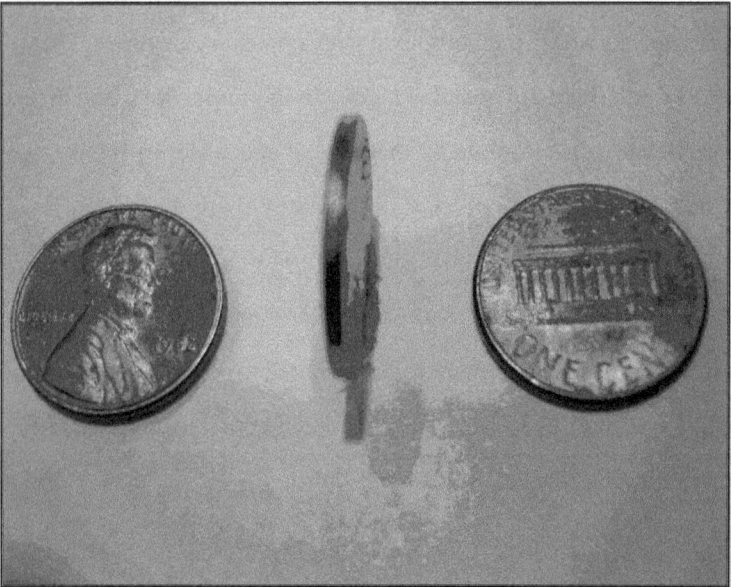

The Blanket

I left the hospital nine days after my eleven-hour operation, with the help of my neighbor, Billy. Diana was attending a "meet the teacher's" night for our high school sophomore, Bryan. She had been with me throughout the entire ordeal, and Billy was more than capable to assist with my departure from the hospital. On the drive home I called Bob, an electrician friend, who was at my house within fifteen minutes to install a cablevision outlet in my "recovery room". We rarely used this room, but this space would be ideal for the sleepless nights and pain-filled days ahead.

I hobbled feebly into the house, sat in my mother-in-law's extra wheelchair, and rolled it into the "recovery room". With what little strength I had, I watched Bob finalize his cable placement, and carefully scrutinized the room where I would spend my next few months. Billy and Bob placed a chair from our upstairs living room into this room. While it looked out of place, the dark blue, worn-in leather recliner that Diana and I had bought as our anniversary present years ago would be cloud-like for my ravaged body.

Diana returned after her conference and we went to bed at about eleven o'clock. I had a short, restless sleep, but I was so comforted in the fact that I was home and that Diana was, at this moment, sleeping soundly at one o'clock in the morning. The weeks of angst had taken their toll on her, and knowing that I was home, our son Bryan was safe, our daughter Laurén was happy in Ecuador, and our other son Michael was comfortable at college, allowed her to grant herself some rest to make up for the lack of sleep she had accumulated over the past month.

I, on the other hand, could not sleep. I crawled out of bed and wheeled myself to the beckoning recliner on the other side of the house. I wanted to reach for a blanket as I left the room, knowing that the recovery room was a little chillier, but my minimal strength and the knowledge that opening the closet would wake Diana prompted me to travel without a cover. At least I had socks on.

The dim hallway light allowed me to see the silhouette of surroundings that I knew well. My recliner, the couch, a Queen Anne chair, and a small table supporting a television were all that occupied this 16' by 16' space just off the kitchen and dining room. I looked around again for a blanket, but found nothing. All I wanted to do at that moment was to sit in the cushioned recliner. A blanket would have made it more comfortable, but required more energy than I could rally. I transferred from the wheelchair to the recliner and leaned back, relaxing as much as my body would allow.

My conversations with God usually begin with a "thank you" for the blessings that I have received. This evening I began the same way, despite my disappointment with my current plight. It didn't take long for me to connect and begin having a very relaxed discussion. Talking to God is like talking to your best friend. I just start talking and the conversation just flows with whatever is on my mind. There is nothing that is out of bounds because He knows what I am thinking about anyway. Sometimes I talk out loud, and sometimes our discussions are all carried out in my head. This evening they were verbal, but quiet enough not to carry to the other side of the house.

I thanked Him for my blessings and my joy of being home, and how wonderful my friends and family had been, even though the whole cancer thing was a pretty big disappointment for all of us. Without blaming Him for causing my cancer, I did make implications as to His ultimate power in directing things, and that my cancer could have been an unnecessary direction for my life. The chill of the room began to hit me and I made a remark that took the conversation in a new direction.

"It would be nice to have a blanket," I mumbled.

"Why don't you ask for one?" was the response from God that had no sound, but answered my question in my head quicker than I could have fashioned the answer to myself.

"Would it fall out of the sky?" I retorted somewhat chidingly.

"Why wouldn't it?" He responded immediately. "You believe that cancer fell out of the sky into your abdomen. Why couldn't a blanket do the same?"

"Well, I believe that the cancer can fall *out* of my abdomen and that You have the power to do that," I said feeling uncomfortable with the intensity of the conversation and getting a little testy with the "Big Guy."

"And yet you think that I have the power to put cancer in your abdomen and not give you a blanket?" He retorted.

"I am not blaming You; I wouldn't blame You for the cancer. However, if you choose to cure me, so be it. I want to believe, and I choose to believe that You have already removed the cancer and will seal the deal with the chemotherapy," I answered carefully. The conversation that had started with the innocent blanket comment had now turned into a questioning link between God's power and my faith.

"Okay, so why wouldn't you believe that I could throw a blanket on you as easily as you believe that I gave you cancer?" God asked me.

"I am not accusing You of the cancer," I repeated sheepishly, even though I believed that He had the power to dispense or eliminate disease.

"Forget the cancer," the voice came back, somewhat annoyed. "Why would you think that I *couldn't* throw a blanket on you?"

"Well, um, I guess You could, but that would be a like a magic trick and I don't think You would do that at two o'clock in the morning," I said, defending my incredulity.

"Do you doubt that I could?" He taunted.

"No, I don't doubt that You could, but I don't think faith necessarily breeds blankets really falling from the sky."

"You see, that's the problem. Your belief systems, and those of most people, say that I cannot and will not throw a blanket on you to comfort you, but you do believe that I freely dispense and disperse cancer and hundreds of other diseases."

At this point, deep into my conversation state, I thought, 'W*ell, maybe there is a blanket and I just didn't see it.'* I had been in this room several times that evening and I knew full well that there had not been a blanket, and there was not one here now. A sheet was occasionally placed on the couch for the dog, but when people were expected, Diana usually took that off and cleaned up the room, which accounted for the room's present blanket-less-ness state. Even with the dim light, I could see clearly that there was no blanket. I scanned the room again through squinted eyes, and felt the back of my chair; still there was no blanket.

So I continued the conversation.

"I am not saying that You can't put a blanket on me or drop one from the sky, but it's uncommon to see blankets falling from the sky, especially in a living room at two a.m., but I certainly believe that you could, and if you choose to do so I would appreciate it. I am certainly not asking for such a service at this time, but I **will** ask that the cancer drops **out** of my abdomen. That's what I want now. However, with that accomplished, it would be nice to have a blanket dropped onto me. As I am cold, I think I am going to go back to the other side of the house and go to bed, if that is all right with you."

More than an hour had passed and I believed the conversation had already touched on what I wanted to discuss. However, He was not done. I leaned forward slowly to get out of the easy chair, and as I did, I noticed a light green fabric peeking out from underneath the corner of the couch. There on the floor lay a clean folded sheet that Diana had hidden there earlier in the day. It was a sheet that she thought she might use during the day as a couch cover for the dog after the company left.

The sheet was just barely within my reach, and I grasped it with my fingertips, carefully pulling it over my body. I smiled as I warmed slightly, acknowledging the big guy's forethought in having Diana place the sheet there. Teasingly, I commented, "But it's a sheet not a blanket."

The humor was evident to me, and as I thanked God for the "cover," I felt Him smile also. After a little more conversing, I shuffled back to my bed where a warm blanket was waiting and God's instrument, my wife, curled into me. I smiled about my communication and contact with a humorous God and believed that He understood my request to be cancer-free just as well as He got my need for a blanket.

Had the story ended there, I would have felt very warm and fuzzy with my conversation about blankets and cancer falling from the sky on my first night home. I felt a strong connection to God and believed that

He was with me.

The next day, I slept soundly. My comfortable bed and warm blanket allowed an entire day to pass with few waking moments. An occasional bathroom run, a piece of toast, and a visiting nurse who changed my dressing, were the only distractions of the day.

The following day, Diana helped me outside. It was a clear September day with cotton ball clouds overhead to temper the warmth of the sun. The light breeze also lessened the late summer heat. Being outside felt wonderful and the fresh air filled my stuffy lungs. Unfortunately, my frail body was beginning to feel chilled, and once again there was no blanket to be had. Diana had gone inside and I was alone with God. It didn't take long to begin a conversation with Him and within seconds, I found myself back on the blanket theme.

At that moment, Bob and Donna, friends of thirty-five years, walked into the backyard and hugged and kissed me. They were the first visitors of the day and I was happy to see them. Bob had been my college classmate, and as close a friend as anyone could ask for. He and Donna married shortly after college and we never lost contact. Donna's claim to fame was her cookies, baked frequently for the newly-graduated college students who had meager jobs and hungry bellies. I was sure that she had brought some cookies and that made me smile.

Seeing their faces warmed my heart, but did nothing for my physical body temperature that was now dropping like a barometer before a storm. The thought of a blanket snuck into my head again as I willed myself to remain focused on the conversation.

"Oh, guess what I brought you!" Donna said enthusiastically. I tilted my head to the right and saw her holding something.

It was a blanket.

"I made you a blanket," she said as she unfurled the fabric. Gracefully it drifted down from the sky and landed atop my body.

"It's warm and lightweight, made out of fleece," Donna said as a smile danced across my face. On one side of the blanket were dolphins jumping across a light blue background, and on the other side was a pattern of the ocean.

As soon as it embraced my body, I felt its softness and warmth penetrate my skin.

"I hope you like it," she said.

I guess blankets do fall out of the sky, I thought to myself, looking heavenward, thanking God for his presence in my life.

"I love it, Donna," I said

Lessons

A conversation with God can occur any time, anywhere. He does not have office hours so there is no need to make an appointment: Just start up a conversation and He will join in.

He does not have an answering machine, and will never put you on hold. He answers the calls Himself.

He is the best therapist you can have. No matter what you may be dealing with, He knows what the real problem is and will direct your attention and help you to find solutions. I thought my problem at that moment was that I needed a blanket. Sure I was cold and a warm cover is what I thought I needed. However, what I really needed was to have strength and faith that God would help me with more than just a chill in my bones.

All we need do is to believe that His power is limitless, and in His own time He will send an angel to deliver His blanket.

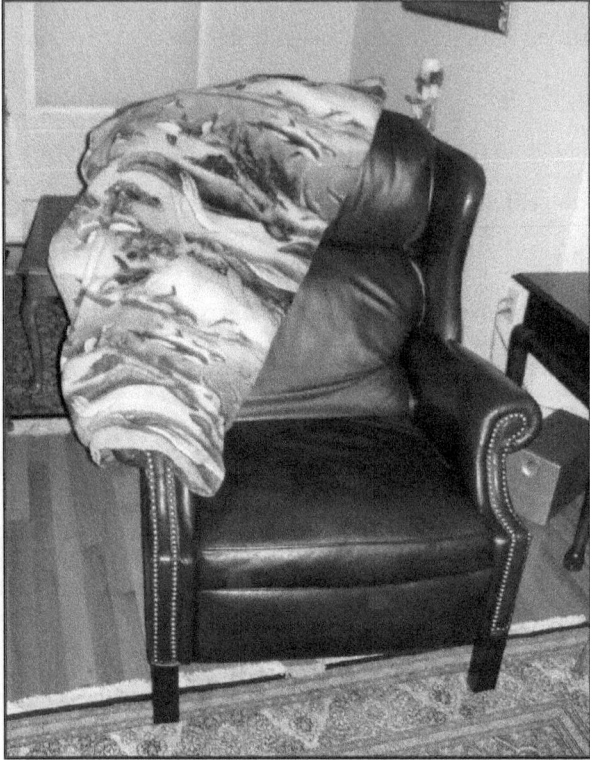

The Blanket

Confusion

At nine a.m., I was scheduled to have a port placed in my chest to make future chemotherapy and blood work less taxing. The device is like a sophisticated tap for extracting sap from a maple tree. A plastic tube inserted into my subclavian vein (near my neck) was to connect to a rubber gasket just below the skin in my chest cavity, where future needles would be placed to access my circulatory system. It sounds worse than it really is.

Anyway, by eleven that morning, I was prepped and ready for the procedure. By this time I had already said goodbye to Diana, who would be waiting for me in the recovery room.

I had shed internal tears on the wheelchair ride down to the surgical room, and even though these somewhat minor procedures were becoming routine, they were still invasive and entailed risk. The nurse was pleasant and our conversation helped to take my mind off of the concerns that hovered around me. This artificial device to be placed within me for months or years felt like yet another violation of my already debased body.

"I'll just park you here for a few minutes," the nurse said as she disappeared through a door not too far down the hundred-foot hallway. I sat alone with my thoughts, staring down the empty space that stretched in front of me. The exit signs were the first things to catch my eye. Their red glow just below the ceiling tiles contrasted the bland beige walls.

The mind can be a dangerous thing when undistracted. If I had a book or a television or something to sidetrack my thoughts, my mind would not have traveled to the exits of life. I began to think about the hallway as life's journey: There are exits in the middle as well as at the end of hallways and life. The exit sign at the end looked so far away and unreachable. And the doors that lined the hallway, where did they go? Did they go to other hallways and have other exit signs along their path? Which door was I going to go through? Who would decide?

The questions were fast and furious. A distraction was necessary. Like a pilot narrowly escaping a tailspin, I looked away from the hall and its exit signs. To my left was a computer station and next to that, a phone on the wall. If I dialed nine, I could probably get an outside line and call someone and talk rather than return my thoughts to the omnipresent red neon signs. I might have even opened solitaire on the unattended computer had a nurse not returned a moment later.

This was a different nurse than the one that had wheeled me to this hallway.

"Hello, I'm Scotty," she said, "and I will be administering the sedation for today's procedure."

"Beam me up Scotty" I replied, and that she did.

An hour later, I was in the recovery room with Diana and the new port in my chest. The grogginess had dissipated and as we left the hospital I could not help but notice the bright red exit signs just below the ceiling tiles. It was okay to follow them and travel through hallways and around corners, down stairs, and out doors. We were headed to Katz's Deli for our traditional post-hospital corned beef sandwich. The sandwich represented a reward for surviving another medical proceedure and brought back fond memories of my youth at the corner deli in Brooklyn.

In reality, following the hospital exit signs did not lead to an untimely end; it was just a new direction and a new beginning.

Lessons

After every red exit sign in the hallway of life, I will forever see a blinking green entry sign. There will always be somewhere to go, and exits are nothing more than alternative paths that allow us to change direction. If you are happy with your life, keep walking down that hallway. If not, choose another corridor. The decisions we make and the journeys we take should be filled with as much laughter, pleasure and love, as possible. Sometimes we need to go through a few doors to find the one that leads to our own personal corned beef sandwich.

My Corned Beef Sandwhich

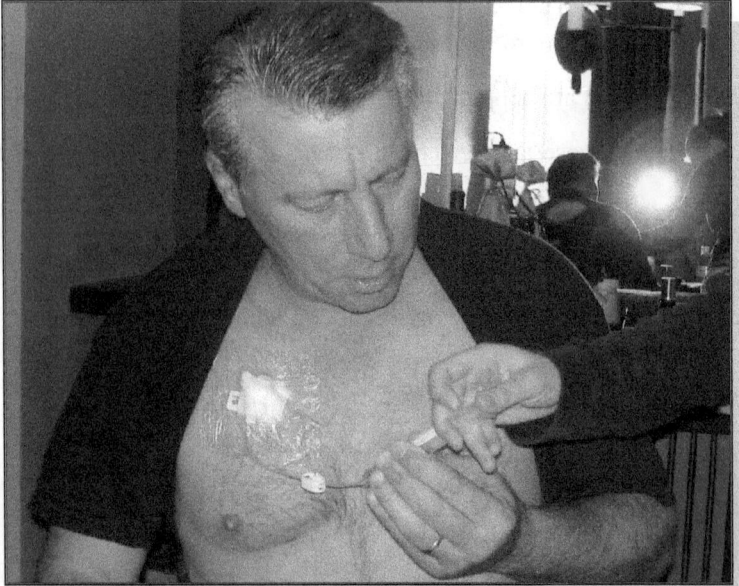

My Last Chemotherapy

My First Chemotherapy

Diana was ready to drive to New Haven with me at seven-thirty for my first intravenous chemotherapy. I had already had three cycles of belly bath chemotherapy, where I was hospitalized for three days at a time and chemicals were infused into my abdomen in order to destroy any remaining cancer cells. Today was to be the first of twelve intravenous treatments, even though I still had three belly baths remaining. Every other weekend from now on, my body would turn into a chemical reservoir. The two different modes of chemotherapy were directed at different areas where the cancer might have spread to. This intravenous attack would hopefully stem any cancerous growth in areas outside of my abdomen.

We were both concerned and slightly worried about this next chapter in the line of body invasions. Would I loose my hair? Would I have discomfort, nausea, diarrhea, or any of the other multitudes of chemotherapy side affects? Would these chemicals kill the remaining cancer cells within me? Would I need more treatments in a year or two? Because of my peculiar type of cancer, the oncologist planned on throwing all sorts of chemicals (Five FU, Oxalyplatin, Lukovoren, and Avastin) in me at the same time. She was unsure of the reactions or the definitive ability of the chemicals in curing me, but she was optimistic. My first day in the "chemo lounge" would last about five hours. I planned to fill my time with writing, reading, and napping.

"Diana, please stay home and get some rest. You can enjoy a beautiful fall day instead of watching chemicals drip into my body," I pleaded.

"No, I need to be there and make sure you do it right," she said.

We both smiled, knowing that she is much better at following directions and would listen closer to the nurse if there were any special instructions. However, after a few more rounds of the conversation, she acquiesced and agreed that I could probably handle the appointment by myself. Her fatigue was obvious, and I was glad that she was persuaded to stay home. She had not slept well since this cancer chapter began, and she would hopefully catch an hour or two of much-needed rest by not accompanying me.

It was noticeably lonely driving to the appointment without her, but I occupied the ten-minute ride with a cell-phone conversation with my friend Ed. He helped to drown out my ominous thoughts of what lay ahead. In reality, I knew that chemotherapy was a routine part of life for thousands of people and that it would probably be no big deal. Diana had seen the chemo room and told me that it looked pretty relaxing: almost party-like with people "hooked up" and talking, reading, or playing cards. Her optimism remained in the back of my mind, but as I walked into the room, I was not looking forward to the day.

Blood work was the first detail at eight-thirty in the morning. I hated blood work and always felt that there should be a better way to access your liquid vitals than puncturing your vein. Oh, that's right, they had come up with a better way: the port in my chest that was already connected to my vein. While it was still somewhat uncomfortable when the nurse accessed the port with a needle in my chest, it was much less annoying than my previous vein-stickings. A straight push with a special needle allowed for a relatively, easy circulatory system access. This unique port device that was surgically embedded into my chest allowed the nurse to see exactly where to place the needle so she was able to access a vein on the first try.

After seeing my oncologist, Dr. Lacey, and her "right arm", Carol, I marched back to the chemo room where I would get my chemicals for the rest of the day. I went there with a smile because Dr. Lacy had not seen anything out of the ordinary in the CT scan from the night before. Even though she had not yet received the radiologist's report, and her reading was not official, it was good enough for me at that moment.

In the chemo room, my nurse Leah connected the tubes and the dripping process began. Less than ten minutes later, Gisela with her warm smile appeared in front of me. In the midst of my experience, her European accent and positive attitude lifted my spirits. She is a massage therapist, and I had heard about her for years from my neighbor Billy, who used her services regularly. "She is great, Bob," Billy would say. In addition to her own massage studio, Gisela offered her services to the oncology unit at Yale Hospital on Tuesdays and Fridays.

There she stood in front of me, and beckoned me to follow her for a therapeutic massage. I looked at Leah, who had just hooked me up to a chemical bag that was connected to my port, and waited for her approval. "Go on," she said, and I got up to follow Gisela, trailing my chemicals on the rolling pole behind me. Gisela positioned pillows so the intravenous needle did not interfere with her therapy, and she began massaging me. Her magic hands made for a thoroughly relaxing half hour.

I filled the following four hours with reading, writing, listening to classical music, and phone calls from Diana. All in all, it was a rather pleasant morning and afternoon. I met some new friends, and saw many people that were hooked up just like me, treating the afternoon not as the be-all, end-all moment of their lives, but as a time to relax and take a break from the day-to-day routine. There was humor, comfort, and warmth between patients and staff, and in that short time span, I saw so much pure love that I was emotionally overwhelmed. If this is chemotherapy, everyone should have a dose of it now and then.

Lessons

As I left the chemo room, I was cleared of trepidation for future treatments. I was concerned about symptoms to come from my infusion of chemicals, but comforted in the feeling that I could find some sweetness in this bowl of lemons.

Seeing people's eyes and hearing the sentiments of their lives that have been turned upside down, puts a new twist on one's perspective of what is important in life. Love, compassion, human kindness, caring for others, respect, and a smile for all is important; everything else is secondary.

If you want to experience a truly eye-opening mind set, sit in the chemo room for a morning. You do not have to get "hooked up", even though it will add to your experience, but just being there will help you see another perspective of life and by so doing, shrink the size of your own personal issues. Your inner warmth will have one less layer to go through to reach the surface.

Choosing a Computer

For three weeks, my son Bryan and I had been going to different computer stores for laptop reconnaissance. I wanted a portable computer to make my hours in the chemo lab productive and constructive. Choices and more choices confused me into leaving multiple stores with a swimming head and no computer. We even consulted my other son, Michael, whose college-world advice was also non-decisive. The choice of a computer is not a life-changing decision, but it weighed heavily on my semi-computer-literate mind. More RAM, better graphics, faster processing, more memory, better sound systems, and a myriad of other alternatives complicated my choice.

By the third time in the same store within three weeks, Bryan had lost his interest in the process. This particular Friday, I had picked up him and his friend Jake from school and we had found our way to the computer section of Best Buy. Forty-five minutes later, I was ready to take the plunge and just buy any computer that seemed, like most of them, to have what I needed. At that moment, Diana called and asked me if I could meet her a few blocks away. Her wallet was in the car that I was driving and she needed her credit card. This gave me a reasonable excuse not to buy a computer at that moment. I told the salesman that I would probably return shortly to seal the deal. The one I'd chosen seemed like a good unit and, after all, it was just a plastic case with memory chips and a keyboard, like all of them. But deep down, I wanted to feel something for the computer to which I would be telling my story. Call me crazy, I was looking for something special.

After dropping off Diana's wallet, the boys and I headed towards home. The boys were done wasting time with indecisive me. However, directly across the street from where I gave Diana her purse was Comp USA: It was another computer store that I had also frequented several times during my search. The car seemed to have a mind of its own as it crossed the four lanes and entered the computer store's parking lot. Bryan and Jake groaned somewhat inaudibly, but humored me by accompanying me to yet another store where we all knew I would become even more frustrated. I was looking at laptop computers for the second time that day, and the eighth time in the past three weeks.

The salesman was pleasant, and after some of the same conversations about RAM, memory, and gigabites, he asked me if I would be interested in a computer that was endorsed by someone with their logo on the case. If that didn't bother me, he said, then it was a great computer that would fit my needs and some of the purchase price would be donated to a worthy cause. Curiously, I followed him around the computer-lined shelves, and there on the end-cap was my computer. It had bright yellow letters that spelled out LIVESTRONG. It was a computer that Lance Armstrong had endorsed, and the salesman did not need to say another word to complete the sale.

Being a cancer survivor and knowing that Lance has done so much to generate funds for cures and promotion of cancer awareness and that some of the purchase price would go to helping the fight against cancer, my search for the right computer ended. Powers beyond my control were tired of seeing me spend hours in confusion, and wasting computer salespeople's time. Now I sit comfortably and confidently typing my story, proud of my technological reconfirmation of God and my ability to LIVE a STRONG life.

Lessons

Ask and ye shall receive. When you are looking for something with your heart, do not doubt that it will come to you – be it a computer, a person, a job, or a wish.

If you put in 90% of the effort, the other 10% will come from powers beyond you.

Dreams

Our dreams can be viewed as portholes to other dimensions. Walk into any bookshop and you will find hundreds of books to interpret your dreams and tell you how they relate to your life. The scientific proof of these interpretations is nonexistent. That does not mean that there is no validity to your dreams providing vision to your life. From this dreamer's perspective, these nighttime mental movies are sometimes for entertainment and sometimes for insight.

I had a dream two nights after the operation. I have always loved my dreams; even the nightmares where I have battled and fought, ones where I was terrified, and of course ones where I was comforted. Several times in my life I have awakened from a dream and not wanted to finish it. I have never seen myself die in a dream, but I have often seen instruments that could end my life. The following dream was as vivid as a "3D" movie in living color and one that I will never forget. It was, I believe, the answer to a prayer.

As the dream begins, I am at my house at the end of a dead-end street, clothed in comfortable, relaxed attire: baggy sweat pants and a t-shirt. I am leaving my driveway and walking toward the main road. Strangely, the road begins to narrow. On the left side of me is the lake on which I live, and on the right are homes that slowly turn into a large wall with gargoyles along its height. The wall is greenish, emerald-like, and gets narrower and flatter as I keep moving onward. It seems to be pressing me closer and closer to the gloomy lake on my left side. Soon, I need to hold on to the cold, convoluted wall, so I do not fall into the water.

Then, as if evolving from the solid wall, a figure appears that resembles a Wookie from Star Wars: huge, hairy, and ominous. He has matted black hair that covers his face and body. His countenance is certainly not appealing, but he does not seem evil. He looks at me with strong eyes that are barely visible behind the hair. Then he beckons me to follow him through the tortuous path that winds along the water's edge. It is my decision to follow him, and I put my faith in this being rather than confronting him and denying his assistance. I am in a strange place and accept the guidance of this unknown.

He helps me through the maze, enabling me to reach the main road where the lake no longer waits to engulf me, and the emerald wall gently fades away. At this point, another one of these beings appears, only larger and more ominous. Without words, they communicate. It seems as though my "guide" informed the other being that he was *letting this one go:* helping it out, helping it through. The other one grunts, looks at me, and then looks away, disappointed in his peer and disinterested in me.

I then come to a large black gate where yet another one of the creatures stands. He is even larger than the previous one. He turns his head and glares at me, and I sense that he is looking into my inner being. He seems cold and distant as his powerful eyes penetrate me. I feel defenseless, yet unafraid.

Smiling, I wordlessly communicate to the being standing in front of the gate that "He helped me through", pointing to the smaller being that stands behind me. The larger one seems to smile, nods his head, and steps aside, allowing me to go through the gate and onto the street where regular people are walking. The sun is shining. The dream is over.

I awoke exhausted, yet invigorated. For the next several hours, I kept pressing the replay button in my mind and I could see the entire dream with clarity as if it were on a DVD being player on a fifty inch plasma television.

Interpreting the meaning of this dream was not difficult from my viewpoint. I had made it through the ugliness of a cancer surgery, the most horrific episode in my life, and I would get through to the other side and rejoin my family. I had put my faith in the hands of a being that was not of an earthly form, and trusted that his guidance would assist me rather than harm me. He was an angel that came to me in a dream to test my faith and subsequently inform me that I would be a survivor. I appreciate and believe the message, and am thankful for the visit.

Lessons

Our dreams are a valuable part of our life and a place where we can connect to the spiritual realm. Some people would say that dreams are just our mind's fantasies, and there is no proof of spirits or angels who communicate with you through this slumber movie. I disagree with them, and am very grateful for this dream that foretold my survival.

My office staff visits me on September 16th: my birthday.

Stevie Z

I graduated dental school thirty years ago, and months later started working for Dr. "B." He had a successful practice in Derby, Connecticut that needed another dentist to assist with the patient load, especially for many of the younger clients. A particular patient will forever remain special as both a patient and a friend.

Stevie Z's mom ushered this affable, blond-haired three-year old into my dental operatory. Behind his brighten-up-your-day smile, little Stevie had considerable amounts of dental decay. Our relationship was obviously strained at times and the necessary work was not always pleasant for Stevie, even with all my compassion, concern, and skill. There is only so much one can do to make "the shot," drilling, and other associated dental trappings somewhat pleasant. He toughed through it, and I admired his brave march in and out of my dental chair on a weekly basis for the fillings.

After two years, I left my job with Dr. "B." and began my own practice in a neighboring town. A year later, Stevie's mom had tracked me down and came to my new office. I never solicited any of the patients I treated at the first office, but if they found me through their own hunting, it was okay and I would treat them. I was happy that they went out of their way to find me, believing that I had touched them in some way. Dr. "B." had hired another dentist, and his practice certainly was not suffering from the few patients that left his care for mine. Stevie Z was one of those disciples who followed me.

Over the next twenty-eight years, Stevie came and went. Sometimes several years would pass between his visits, and unfortunately his dental health always needed repair. Even though he was a conscientious student of the brush (not the floss), his genetic makeup and dietary mistakes (soda and candy) created the ideal environment for dental decay and breakdown. So, repeatedly Stevie would sit back, and I would perform the necessary dental work to keep him healthy.

Several years ago, Stevie came in and was saddened by the death of his father. Like an old friend and someone important in his life I spent some time listening to his grief after I fixed one of his teeth. He had become a young adult and even though, in my eyes, he was still little Stevie Z, I could see his maturation unfold before me. He took his father's passing in a unique spiritual way and felt as though his dad was still with him in his heart.

A few years after that, he was proud to inform me that he had opened up his own pizza restaurant, and more importantly, was married and the father of a baby girl. He even brought his daughter to the office so I could see her.

The day before my cancer surgery, Stevie came in for what would be his last visit. The staff knew what was going on with my health, but no patients were informed. That Monday I was only seeing four patients and would be done by noon.

Stevie Z called that morning in dental pain, and my receptionist Sue asked me if we could see him. As usual, I said "yes", even though I was anxious to put down the drill and go home. He would be my last patient that day. Within half an hour, Stevie assumed his patient position in the chair, and we reminisced a bit before addressing his dental problem.

While the anesthesia was taking effect, he informed me that this would probably be his last visit to my office because he was moving his family to South Carolina. I could barely get a word in edgewise while he told my assistant and me how special I was and how meaningful I had been in his life.

Steve, in my mind, represents my entire dental practice. This child-turned-boy-turned-man was so proud of his dental health. He had become a flosser and a brusher and even bleached his teeth to add more sparkle to his smile. The particular tooth of that day's visit was of no great loss for either of us, but in essence would make his mouth healthier with its removal. I extracted the destroyed lower-right second molar, and he was very thankful that it was a relatively comfortable episode. He was also thankful for the years that I had taken care of him.

His "Thank you's" moved me more than he knew. I escorted him to the front desk and said, "Stevie, that one's on me," waving off any payment for the procedure. My decision not to charge him for the extraction made him smile and made me smile too. I went back into my office after shaking his hand, and sat down thinking that he was the last person that I would see before I went under the blade the next day - how appropriate.

As I shut my eyes for a brief moment of respite within my private office, there was a tap on the door. My dental assistant asked me if I would come out to the front desk because Stevie wanted to say one more thing to me. Slowly, I lifted myself out of the chair and went to the front.

"Dr. Rauch," said Stevie, the thirty-plus-year-old patient of mine in front of five or six of my staff members, "can I give you a hug?" In years of practice I had had patients thank me, hug me, bring me cookies, and write me thank you notes; however, nothing will ever mean as much to me as Stevie asking me for a hug at that moment in time.

I stepped forward and hugged him. He gave me more in his warm, strong embrace than he could have imagined. We both smiled and parted. I went back into my private office still enclosed in Stevie's hug. That hug told me that every patient whom I had treated over the thirty years of my practice was giving me the warmth, compassion, love, and power to help me through my surgery. Stevie Z represented every patient I had ever seen. He had given me a power hug from thousands of people, as I saw it.

Hugs are powerful therapy, and that one was atomic.

A week after my surgery, I saw the surgeon who saved my life. I was now the patient in his arms, and I was the one who wanted to hug him. I asked him, after thanking him, why he took eleven hours to clean me out when he could have conceivably done it in five or six. His thoroughness and painstaking, meticulous cleansing had been instrumental in saving my life. In a soft-spoken voice with a half smile he said, "You'd do the same for me, wouldn't you?"

Stevie Z flashed in my mind and I smiled and said, "Yes I would."

Lessons

Give the world your best and that is what the world will return to you.

"Do unto others as you would have them do unto you." There is no better way to say it. By living with that quotation firmly embedded in your daily life, you can never go wrong.

Hugs are powerful therapy. They are easy to share, cost you nothing, and are more valuable than you can imagine.

God
Ends a Conversation

Finally, all of the holes in my body were closed: The 50 midline stitches were done draining; the belly ports had healed; and the multiple puncture holes for drawing blood and inserting drugs into the bloodstream had closed as well. My thrill for that evening would be climbing into my hot tub, and soaking in the physical relief it provided. My muscle aches and pains from months of abuse would certainly benefit from the warm water and powerful jets. My mind and spirit would also get some relief by sitting outside on a starlit night and conversing with God. I had asked Diana and Bryan if they wanted to join me, but they were busy. So there I sat looking heavenward, and I began a conversation with the night sky.

Soon enough I was rambling once again. As usual, I began my chat by thanking God for all of my previous blessings, and reconfirming my faith in Him despite my current cancer battle. The talk continued for about thirty minutes, filled with words of my passed loved ones, future desires, and well wishes for those who needed them.

The next day I was scheduled for a CT scan, which would examine the abdominal cavity for any remaining or, God forbid, multiplying cancer cells. If there were visible signs of new cancerous growth, then I had big plans to call all of my friends with an open invite to start drinking heavily. Even though I did not consider that a possibility, there was that unavoidable percentage of fear and doubt in my mind. So at this point during my dialogue with God, I focused on my own personal desires.

Some tears welled up and I began by restating that I was totally in awe of His power and would respect whatever His plans might be. Who was I to alter them? But if it was in any way possible, I would like to see a clear CT scan and confirmation that, at least for now, the cancer was under control. As I looked up to the sky, I then affirmed my personal belief that I would be much more valuable on this planet for the next thirty to forty years than wherever else I might go after leaving my body. I believe that we are spiritual beings and that when we leave our body, the game of our life is not over. I am not sure exactly what happens, but I do have ideas and they are all good. Many religions have laid out scenarios for the afterlife, leading us to believe that "the game" is not over when our spirit leaves our body.

Throughout the hot tub talk, I had been feeling pretty good vibrations and feedback as to the Big Guy's responses. When I asked for things to go right for the fifth or sixth time, a shooting star blasted above me. It streaked across the sky from left to right and glowed brighter as it sped along. It was not the kind of shooting star that I had seen on other nights from the corner of my eye, or the kind that seemed so far away that it really didn't count. This was a bright, full-view shooter that I saw, from its birth to its passing. And when it ended, it seemed to light up in a large circle and then turn dark. For those two seconds, my entire being was captivated with the sight. Then, looking into the blackness that had been the shooting star, I smiled. For me, this was the end of that conversation with God. In His most magnificent way, in my mind at least, He had informed me that He would consider my request positively, and that our dialogue had finished for the night. Now that's one great way to end a conversation.

Lessons

The next day I had the CT scan, and there were no signs of recurrence. Unfortunately, I will have CT scans periodically for the rest of my life; the seeds of worry may pervade my thoughts, but I will always remember that on the night before my first one, my conversation ended with a stellar wink from God, promising that everything was okay.

None of my conversations with God have ever ended so dramatically. I assume that because my emotion was so elevated, He needed to really communicate His participation in our conversation. Surely, I could be reading into a shooting star all sorts of messages when, after all, it is, according to many people, just a meteorological event without any spiritual component. Not for me. That shooting star was truly spiritual and that's the way I will always see it.

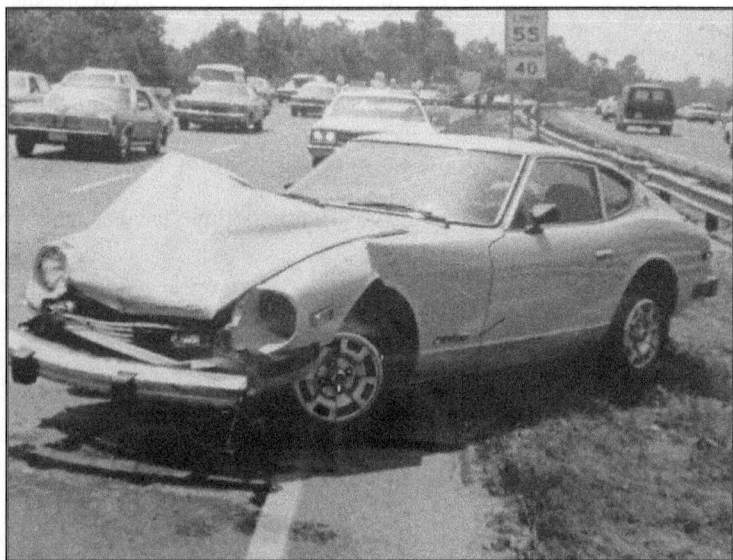

My First 280Z Collision

PART TWO:
LIFE STORIES BEFORE CANCER

Before cancer, I was introduced to life
lessons that proved invaluable in my quest
to cope with burdens that often seemed
insurmountable. These lessons were
sometimes couched in near disaster; other
times they occurred during pivotal moments
where my decision would determine my future.
During the battle with cancer,
I often reflected on these experiences and
gleaned strength and wisdom from them.
The following vignettes are some of
the most dramatic episodes from which I
learned priceless lessons that continue
to help me survive.

1964 Galaxy 500xl Convertible

Galaxy 500

The 1964 blue-green Galaxy 500xl convertible was the perfect car for what Andy, my freshman roommate, liked to call "mystery trips". Andy would wake me up singing the mystery trip song. (*We're goin' on a mystery trip, a mystery trip, a mystery trip. We're goin' on a mystery trip, a mystery mystery mystery mystery mystery mystery trip*), whereupon we would hop into the Galaxy 500 convertible and go. Our thirst for adventure, combined with Andy's seemingly limitless family cash flow, allowed us some wonderful weekend adventures: Boston for a Jethro Tull concert; New York for *Jesus Christ Super Star* (front row tickets); and even just going left or right for an entire day and ending up somewhere far from home, needing to find our way back late at night.

This particular mystery trip proved to be a pivotal one for my future viewpoint on life. It was the spring of 1969 and we were freshman at the University of Bridgeport in Bridgeport, Connecticut. We were both pre-med majors, and this was a well-known school for its ability to matriculate its students into top medical and dental schools. Its rural setting and lighter congestion allowed us to feel as though the open road was without restrictions. This particular Saturday morning found Andy and me "heading left", and before long we found the Sikorsky Airport in Bridgeport. We sat next to the runway and watched the planes land and take off as we laughed and talked about the meaning of life, how our futures would unfold, and who would buy the beer for the weekend.

After an hour or two, we got back into the car and left the airport. As we reached the end of the access road, Andy stopped at the stop sign, and then he proceeded to take a left onto the main road. The Galaxy was going about 15 miles per hour by the time it was in the middle of the intersection. Then, from the left corner of my left eye, I saw the car that would collide with us. It was cruising towards us on the main road at about 65 miles per hour. From 100 yards away, even with slammed brakes, the cars could not help but impact each other. The front of his car hit the left front of ours, almost head-on at a combined speed of nearly 60 miles per hour.

As I realized how the cars would crash, (doing the high school math of two approaching cars traveling at the combined speed of 60 mph colliding head on from a distance of 55 yards, the time of impact equals 1.7 seconds), my mind told my body that I had only seconds to live. Without a seat belt I would be thrust through the windshield and my life would be over.

I had never been a firm believer in any of the packaged religions, but I did not discount that there may be some truth to their theories. My skepticism had allowed me to think about, ponder, and discuss spirituality, but never commit to any of their beliefs as being fact. There was never enough evidence scientifically to convert me to believing that faith was proof of anything, yet, at this moment, I would forever be changed as far as faith was concerned. Many people have faith without the trauma of a life threatening episode, but what happened next made a believer out of me. From that moment on, I would be convinced that our bodies are just vessels housing our immortal spirit.

It has been said that your life flashes before your eyes in times like this. **It does.** During those 1.7 seconds, the noise of the screeching tires seemed to fade away to a distant background becoming bland and inoffensive. The car before me seemed to stop and proceed like flashes of an old movie, each frame distinct and separate. With each image, the cars moved a fraction of distance closer until impact. Then the approaching car faded to the background and three-dimensional pictures of my childhood flashed in space. They were not in sequential order necessarily, but in random patterns with friends of mine, my parents, my brother, my home, and of things that were important to me. The images encapsulated my short eighteen years of life before my eyes on a strip of thin air.

I seemed to be outside of my physical body, above and behind myself, watching my muscles brace themselves as credits of my life rolled by. There was no fear attached to this; as a matter of fact, there was no emotion at all. I felt more like a distant observer than a participant in the accident. Then I saw my body thrust forward as the cars impacted. My head smashed into the windshield. My arms, elbows first, hit the dash board and my knees careened into the glove compartment. As I said before, we were not wearing seat belts.

What must have been a loud, crashing noise, did not register with my senses. I watched my body thrust to the right, hit the door, lean back against the seat, and then bound to the left into Andy's flying body. Again I headed towards the dashboard and stopped my motion with my hands, nearly breaking wrists as they bent backwards. The vehicles let out one last sigh and came to rest. Similar to a theater after the movie, all went dark.

When the lights came on, I instantly re-entered the body that was now at rest. Like the *Starship Enterprise* jumping into light speed, the speck of me that was watching the episode from the near distance surged into my bodily frame once again. My mental, physical, and spiritual selves had rejoined. As my eyes opened, I saw the smashed glass, the steaming engine, and the backdrop of the world around me. I looked to the left and met Andy's eyes. He was okay and so was I, and so was the driver of the other car. We were all bloody and banged up, but we were all alive.

Our trip to Bridgeport Hospital confirmed that we would recover, and with some doctoring, we were allowed to go back to our dormitory. The Galaxy 500, unfortunately, was dead.

LESSONS

In 1968, out-of-body experiences were rarely discussed. Hallucinogenic drugs and abundant alcohol were used to achieve what people believed were out-of-body experiences. This accident was a spiritual awakening for me. I now have faith that there is life after we shed our physical body, as well as the fact that God exists and is watching over us. That faith has been a major part of my life, and I am thankful for that near-death experience that allowed me to see clearly what is real to me now.

Addendum:
Another Mind-Body-Spirit Divergence

Eleven years after my near-death, out-of-body experience, while Diana and I were planning our wedding, her father, Steve, had checked himself into the hospital for chest pains. When we went to visit him, he had a heart attack right in front of us. Within seconds, the efficient staff at Griffin Hospital had the paddles on him and he was revived.

I was the first to talk to Steve. He revealed that he had been heading towards a bright light and it had been beautiful. For some reason, he had turned back and did not ascend. He had been a church-going man before this experience, but after it, his life took on an entirely new perspective. From then on, his glass was more often half-full as opposed to half-empty. His doctors said that he only had one year to live with his damaged heart and there was little that could be done for his condition. Faith was his cure, and he outlived his doctor's prediction for another seventeen years.

My father-in-law passed away in 1995. At the funeral, a close friend of his approached Diana and told her a story that Diana's dad had related about his heart attack seventeen years earlier. The friend told Diana that the reason her dad had turned away from the light was that he had heard Diana's voice calling, "Daddy, I need you. Come back to me. Come back to me. Please, do not go." Diana had been the only person in the room at that moment in time, as I had been running down the hallway shouting for help. Diana was the only one privy to what she'd said that day and now her words were repeated back to her seventeen years later. When Diana heard the words that she had yelled to her father, tears streamed down her face, knowing that her father chose to stay alive for her.

The night before her father's final heart attack, Diana had spoken with God. Her father looked tired, weak, worn, and had not been feeling well for a while. She told God she knew her dad had suffered and if it was his time, it was okay to take him. The next morning, her father saw the white light again and peacefully followed wherever it led.

It was Steve's initial decision to turn away from the beckoning light and be with his family for many years. During that time, he managed to resurrect a beautiful relationship with his family, see his grandchildren, and reconfirm **my** faith in the heavens above. When God called him again, he was ready to go.

Lessons

I thank God every day that I am alive, and I know that the inevitability of death can be a second away, a foot away, or as far away as the voice of a loved one.

I believe that:

There is spiritual life after physical death.

We have some control as to when our spiritual self departs our physical body.

We are all spiritual beings residing temporarily in physical bodies.

Love is the most powerful force we have to control our destiny. Diana's love for her dad and his love for her enabled him to postpone the unavoidable for seventeen more years.

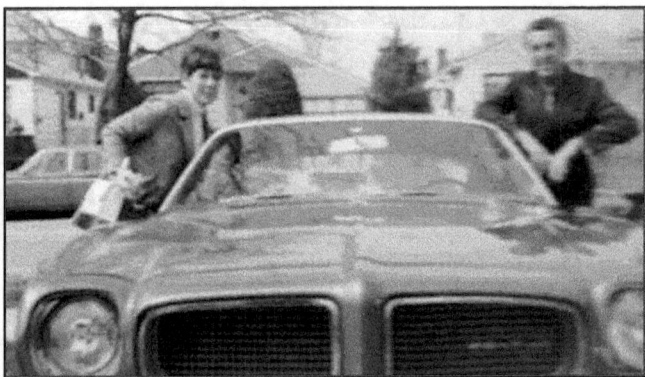

My mom and dad and my new Firebird

Motivation

"So how are you enjoying college, Bob?" my dad asked.

"Fine, Dad. Everything is going fine."

I was a freshman at the University of Bridgeport, in Bridgeport, Connecticut, which had an outstanding reputation. Its exceptional biology department would act as a stepping stone for medical school. My parents thought that I would be a great doctor and directed me that way. I was a relatively intelligent person and thought it seemed like a good idea also.

"So you have been winning, Bob?" My dad said with conviction.

"What do you mean, Dad?"

"You have been winning, right?" My dad repeated.

Growing up in Brooklyn, my poker playing had been seen as the lesser of other evils, so my dad had condoned card playing throughout my high school years.

"You have been winning, haven't you?" he repeated, patiently.

"Why would you say that, dad?" I responded sheepishly

"You haven't cashed a check in two months."

I was busted. How could I be so dumb as to not cover my tracks? For most of my freshman year, the money I won at poker came before school and before grades. At the end of my first semester, my grade point average (GPA) was only a 1.74, but I had won a few hundred dollars.

Considering that the minimum entrance GPA for medical school was a 3.3 at the time, things did not look good for my future as a doctor. The dean of the biology department had called me in and recommended that if I had any hopes for medical school, I should leave his department and just take the necessary biology requirements as electives. Hopefully, I would get better grades as a psychology major and raise my GPA to a more respectable range.

During the second semester of my freshman year I maintained my lackluster performance; however, I did improve to a 2.4. Averaging my freshman grades together left me far below the necessary 3.3 needed to enter any medical school. A 2.0 would not get me far.

When my brother (four years my senior) was a college sophomore, my dad bought him a car so that he could get to and from college and move another step along on the road to maturity. As I approached my sophomore year, I asked my dad what vehicle I could get. I had already accumulated brochures from every dealer available and had set my sights on a new 1970 Pontiac Firebird. I had chosen a bright blue finish with a 350 engine and racing mirrors. This was going to be the best toy I had ever gotten. My future as a physician mattered very little compared to the Firebird.

"So you want a Firebird, Bob?"

"Yes, Dad."

"What will it cost?" he asked.

I had the figures right in front of me with everything I wanted.

"It costs thirty-six hundred dollars, Dad." I responded.

My Dad was not a wealthy man, but he was capable of providing me with that vehicle even though retrospectively I'm sure it strained his pocketbook.

"Fine, Bob. That's what you want, well here's the deal: Whatever you get for a grade point average your first semester as a sophomore, that's what we will spend on your car. If you get a 4.0 then you can have four thousand dollars towards your car. If you get a 3.6, well there's your Firebird. And if you get a 1.75, like you got freshman year, then seventeen hundred and fifty dollars is all you'll have towards your car."

My freshman grades would probably buy me a stripped-down Volkswagen. A 3.6 would get me my Firebird. But that was impossible - almost straight A's! I really had no negotiating power in this deal, but shook my Dad's hand anyway, smiling. I was bluffing both him and myself by thinking that I could really get a 3.6 average.

Knowing the way the system worked, I made a couple of calls and found out what classes I should take: the *gut* courses, the easy ones, the ones that could get me the A's I needed.

First semester sophomore year found me taking Music Appreciation, Art History, French 101 (for the second time), and two basic Psychology courses where the professors were known to give out A's even if you didn't attend class. I had switched my major from biology to psychology, and I knew that after this semester I would have to load up on some biology courses in order to fulfill the pre-med requirements.

That was a far off dream and I doubted, as did most of my friends and the chairman of the biology department, that I could ever pick my GPA up to med-school range. Deep down, I'm sure my heart was not dedicated to being a physician. I believed I had a calling for the medical field, but a physician's control of another's life and death seemed too much for my emotional constitution to handle. I was 19 years old and headed on a path, but all that mattered then was getting my 3.6 and my Firebird.

The first semester of my sophomore year I limited my gambling to the weekends so that I would have some spending cash for the week. The rest of the time I buckled down to school work. Sure enough, at the end of the semester, I had attained a 3.6. As soon as my grades appeared, I handed them to my dad, and he called up the automobile dealer. The car was delivered six weeks later.

The keys were almost in my hands and the bright shiny blue Firebird sat there ready for me to embrace. Then my dad dropped the bomb, a crushing blow, the wake up call.

"Bob," my Dad said as he smiled at me, "you had a great semester and I am proud of you. Now I know that you have the potential to do anything you want and to get any grade that you need in order to pursue a career. The fine print of our agreement, before I hand you these keys, is that if you ever get below a 3.6, I will repossess your car and return it to the dealer."

"What?" I heard myself say as my throat choked. He repeated himself: "If you get below a 3.6, you lose your car, you lose your wheels, and the bus will be the mode of your transportation for the rest of your college life."

"That's a little harsh, Dad."

"Well, it's clear to me that you can get the grades and obvious what motivated you."

"But...."

"You want the keys, then that's the deal," he said with a dry smile. My dad was a businessman, and he knew how to wheel and deal. I knew that I would never hold a candle to him if this was a poker game. He had a full house, and I had a pair of nothings.

"Okay," I said, as my smile turned to ultimate worry. Conceptually, I would only have this car for one semester unless I could find more easy courses to take. Or I could really study to get the grades I needed. The amazing thing about our abilities is that until they are tested, we really don't know what we've got.

I returned to school and once again asked around about who the easy professors were and how I could get easy classes for good grades. The upperclassman laughed at me and said I had taken all of them in the last semester: It was time to buckle down. The only way to get a 3.6 or better for the rest of my college career was to actually work.

The short version of the next three years of college: I kept that Firebird, and received the highest grade in organic chemistry, physics, biochemistry, genetics, and every psychology class I took. I had the intelligence, and now I had the motivation. By senior year, I had picked up my overall grade point average to a 3.2, and had realized my full potential as a student.

Lessons

At nineteen years old, I learned that the proper motivation at the proper time can bring out the best in a person. I know I can perform or do just about anything I want to. I am capable, able, and I respect myself enough to know that I can turn on the *afterburners* and get the most out of me if I put my mind to it. The Nike motto, "Just do it," is real. I have seen it. I have lived it. If the poker player from Brooklyn can "do it," I know anyone can.

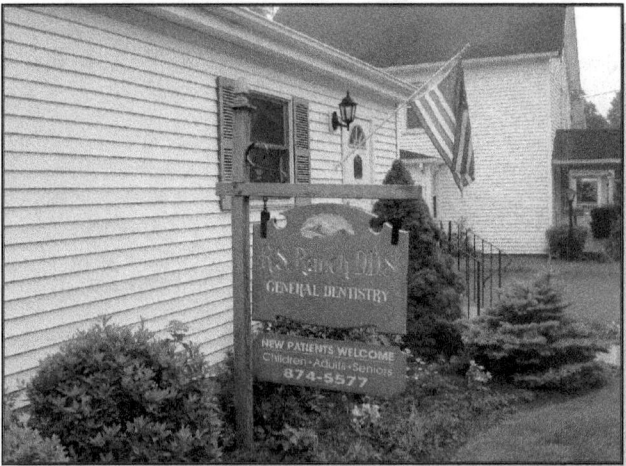

Motivated And Waiting

During my studious years of college, I realized that even though I enjoyed biology, traditional physician-type medicine did not entice me. In the middle of my senior year, my roommate Andy suggested that I visit with his uncle David, the dentist. I had never considered the profession of dentistry; however, after I talked with David I liked it immediately. I saw what he did with his hands to provide an extraordinarily useful medical service to patients without the urgency of life and death. He was a master in one of the healing arts, and he made people smile and improved their self-esteem while improving their physical health. His days were filled with different people and creative ways to reconstruct and repair their dental health. He also had the ability to educate others and to prevent disease. This profession seemed ideal for my abilities; unfortunately, it was December when I figured out what I wanted to be. In order to apply to dental schools I still needed to take the dental board examinations. Consequently, schools received my applications in March, after they had already chosen most of their incoming classes.

In April of my senior year, rejection notices from the medical schools floated in like the rising tide at the water's edge. Even though my 3.2 average was enough to get me into medical school and my medical entrance exams were also in the acceptable range, the pool of applicants that year made my "average application" look just that: average. With many higher-rated applicants to choose from, I was just another pretty face with nothing exceptional to offer.

The med school rejections didn't bother me that much, because by this time I was pretty well convinced that dentistry was my calling.

Disappointment started to hit me when the rejections from the dental school began. The chairman of the biology department (the same man who suggested that I leave his department) explained to me that the lateness of my applications for dental school and the lateness of my January dental examinations had put me in a pool of applicants that were less likely to be accepted. Most of the class for the coming semester had already been chosen before my applications had ever reached the dental school's doorsteps. I did receive two interviews however, which translated into possible acceptances to New York University (NYU) and Georgetown University.

That spring I interviewed at NYU and blew it. When I left that day from the interview, I knew the rejection notice would be waiting on my doorstep when I got home. A month later I had an interview at Georgetown Dental School and I nailed it. I was confident, prepared, and the three professors with whom I spoke were very pleased with my performance. A week later I received notification that I had made it to their "waiting list". I had graduated the University of Bridgeport with a degree in Psychology, a minor in Biology, and my only future prospect at that moment was the waiting list at Georgetown University Dental School.

To ignore the reality of no definitive future direction, I worked that summer at a camp in upstate New York, as I had for the previous two summers. I was a legendary boating counselor at Camp Natchez near the Berkshire Mountains. It was an entertaining summer, but a rather anticlimactic end to four years of college.

The phone call from my dad the last week of camp was rather bizarre: "Bob, have you heard anything from Georgetown?"

"No dad. Did I get any mail at home?"

"No. You're still on the waiting list, aren't you?"

"Yeah, I guess so."

"When does school start down there?"

"I think in a week or so."

"Well, I'll tell you what."

"What?"

"You're coming home in a few days, right?"

"Yes."

"Well, as soon as you get home, I'll pay you a hundred dollars a week plus expenses and you go down to Georgetown and wait."

"What do you mean, 'wait'?"

"Well, you're on the waiting list, so go down to the dean's office, introduce yourself, and wait."

"Wait for what?"

"Well, wait to get into dental school."

The hundred dollars and the fact that I had nothing better to do motivated me to say, "Sure, I'll go wait."

So, I drove home from camp, repacked my Firebird, drove to Washington, D.C. the next day, and checked into a hotel just across the Key Bridge from the Georgetown campus.

At 8 a.m. that Monday morning, I entered the dental school and introduced myself to the secretary of the dean. She acknowledged that I was on the waiting list, and after some small talk, she informed me that there was no order as to who would be chosen from the waiting list, or, if in fact another student would be. She explained that the entire class had already been chosen. All the students had paid their tuition and started classes that day, and there was no room for another student. They would gladly call someone from the waiting list pool if another spot became available.

With a mild, "Thank you," and a slight smile, I walked back several paces and sat in a chair. Then, I opened a book that I had recently started: J.R.R. Tolkien's *The Return of the King*, the third book in his "Lord of the Rings" trilogy. Her quizzical look is a fond memory. Without giving her time to ask what I was doing, I simply looked up, smiled and said, "If it's okay with you, as long as I'm on the waiting list, I'll just sit here and wait."

Lunchtime came and passed, students came and passed, the gentleman whom I assumed to be the dean came and passed, and eight hours later, the secretary who was now my quasi-friend was ready to pass through the door and end her day. She held the door open for me to leave.

"I'll see you tomorrow," I said.

Again her quizzical look begged for an answer.

"I'll be waiting," I said.

That night I was alone and questioned why I was there. The class was full, the hundred forty-two students had chosen their career, selected the school, and paid their money. Why would any of them change their minds now?

I drove around Washington and ended up at the Lincoln Memorial where I sat on the steps, walked around its perimeter and read the speeches on the walls. I found myself alone, talking to old Abe as he sat there, solid, stoic, and powerful.

What Abraham Lincoln had confronted was unimaginable. The

Civil War, the Emancipation Proclamation, his rise to respected leadership, and the shaping of a great nation were inspirational and motivated me to continue my waiting with renewed vigor. It must have been two or three o'clock in the morning when I realized that Abe, the security guard, and I were the only ones there. I went back to the hotel, invigorated and hopeful of one spot opening up for Georgetown's Dental School

My alarm went off and I made it to the dental school even before the secretary opened the door to the dean's office.

"Good morning," I said as I, took my seat, crossed my legs, and began waiting. This time she didn't even bother to try to dissuade me, or tell me that they would "call me." She knew my determination, and she knew I was going to sit there. Most of the morning was full of considerable action back and forth within the dean's office. The dean and what appeared to be several professors walked by and glanced at me several times. The secretary had handed them some papers, then continued her daily chores of answering the phones.

At one o'clock she came to me and said, "You can go to lunch now."

"I'll wait."

"No, please. Go to lunch," she repeated. Her eyes glistened and she smiled slightly. I was hungry, so I went nearby to the hospital cafeteria, ate a quick hot dog, and returned within thirty minutes to continue my waiting. After my time spent at the Lincoln Memorial I somehow believed that I would be accepted to this dental school and would become a dentist. I believed in my heart that I was capable and that dentistry was the right profession for me.

I entered the waiting room and took my seat.

"That was a quick lunch!" the secretary said.

"Well, I am pretty committed to this waiting business, you know."

She smiled then went back to doing her work, and I went back to my book. About an hour later, the gentleman who I believed to be the dean walked out and stood directly in front of me.

"Bob Rauch," he said, "I'm Dean Emig, the dean of the dental school." He held out his hand, which I acknowledged by holding out my own hand and standing up. He looked me up and down and then directly into my eyes. Then, with all seriousness, he said, **"I'm sorry."**

The deafening silence allowed me to hear my heart fall on top of my foot and roll to the ground. Lucky for me, my seasoned poker face did not show the ultimate disappointment that I felt.

His timing, however, was impeccable. He waited about three seconds and then said, **"But..."**

My heart rolled back up onto my foot and started to slowly ascend, reaching almost my knee as another three seconds went by.

"I'm sorry, but..." the sentences joined together in my mind.

"But, you're in!" he continued.

Putting the sentence together, I finally heard it: *"I'm sorry, but you're in."* My heart jumped back into place and my confused look turned into a smile that split my face in half.

I could see the secretary behind him beaming.

"I'm in?" I stammered.

"Yes," he chuckled. "but you've missed two days of classes. Sherry, my secretary, will go over the necessary paperwork. You will be expected in class at eight o'clock tomorrow morning."

At that moment a student walked into the office wearing a white dental outfit. Dr. Emig turned around and looked at him.

"Tom," he said.

"Yes," replied the student.

"This is Bob Rauch. He was just accepted to the dental school, and I'd like you to look out for him," Emig said with conviction.

"Fine," Tom responded. Tom was a sophomore, and for the next three years he would be my "big brother". He was like an angel in a white dental coat who was helpful in so many ways during that part of my life.

Apparently, one student had gotten accepted to another dental school and decided to leave Georgetown at the last minute. My being there and having the necessary qualifications got me that spot: **the last spot**.

I called my dad from the nearest phone and shared my elation. "Congratulations, Robert. We'll see you this weekend and have everything you need ready to go."

I went to class the next three days and drove home that Friday afternoon for the weekend before I would return to Georgetown and start my dental career. I lived with Tom for a few weeks, until I was able to find myself an apartment. Many nights found me at the Lincoln Memorial after studying or after the library had closed.

At the beginning, I was a little worried because the students were from many prestigious schools around the country, and I was unsure if I really had made the grade or had just gotten lucky. Was I able to perform up to the level of these students?

The first exam in dental materials was supposedly the hardest that dental students would ever take. The two hundred-question, multiple choice test three weeks after the first day of school was the one that separated the men from the boys. I got the fourth highest mark in the class and never worried again if I had what it took to make it through the next four years.

Four years later my mom, dad, and brother sat in the audience and watched me get my dental diploma.

Lessons

I have been a practicing dentist for over thirty years. I have treated over seventy-five thousand patients, and most of my work remains healthy and functional. The profession of dentistry is absolutely the right profession for me. It is strange how I was guided towards this career and how my entrance into dental school required my own fortitude, coupled with my dad's suggestion to "Go down and wait". Life is funny the way it unfolds: If you follow a path and allow things to ebb and flow, you might just be surprised and get what you wished for.

Diana

My close friends Douglas, Ricky and I left my apartment on December 30, 1978 at four o'clock in the morning headed for Killington, Vermont. The four-hour ride from Hamden, Connecticut would get us there at eight a.m. We would have breakfast and be the first ones on the slopes. We had been the last ones to leave a local pub the night before, but still managed to sleep for a few hours before starting our trip. Ricky was my passenger in the bright yellow Datsun 280Z sports car with RSR-DDS license plates. Douglas, Ricky's older brother, was following us in Ricky's brand new black Firebird. Life was good, and I was "living large". I had graduated Georgetown Dental School single and carefree a year and a half before. I had friends, money, vacations to Club Med, weekend parties, and a nice apartment that acted as a place to sleep and change my clothes whenever I wasn't gallivanting around New England.

At almost double the speed limit on Route 91 north, I hit a patch of black ice just south of Springfield, Massachusetts. The slow left bend in the road teased the car out of my control, and allowed the rear tires to drift towards the right lane. Riding through the skid was an emotionless moment and Ricky and I braced for what was sure to be a 100 mph impact with the right side guard rail, head on. The beautiful thing that I later found out about Datsun 280Z's was that the long nose, which was all engine, had been designed so that in the case of a head-on collision, the entire engine would hit a slanted steel plate and direct the engine downward and underneath the vehicle. The long nose would crumple and soften the impact, leaving its seat-belted passengers uncrushed.

The explosive crash deafened our ears as our bodies gyrated whichever way Newtonian forces directed them. When the car came to rest, Ricky and I were physically unharmed. In a shocking moment, we smiled broadly at cheating death, only to realize that Douglas had hit the same ice patch with his Firebird. Fortunately for Doug, he hit the brakes, and slowed his car after seeing our skid. His crash pattern was similar to ours and we saw him heading towards Ricky's door.

Doug spun out of control. We braced ourselves and hoped that his car did not end up in Ricky's lap. Fortunately for all of us, he stopped inches before slamming into my already totaled Datsun. The three of us jumped out of the cars, ran up the road, and started flagging down anyone that might be coming our way so that they could avoid the ice patch as well as our sitting-duck cars. It was not even five o'clock in the morning, so there were just a handful of cars on the road. In less than thirty minutes, state troopers, local police, towing vehicles, flares, and firemen blanketed the area. By ten in the morning, the Firebird was somewhat serviceable, so we piled everything into his trunk and continued our journey northward. My car was totaled and remained behind at some Springfield auto shop.

I would call my auto dealer, Leonard, in Hamden, Connecticut later that day to tell him where my car was so he could handle the paperwork and do whatever they do with destroyed vehicles. There was no reason to cancel our ski weekend. Physically, we were fine, and the fresh air and workout would help to clear our minds from the trauma. We skied the afternoon at Okemo Mountain and that night we drove Ricky's traumatized Firebird to Killington, our original destination, and stayed at some lackluster motel. It rained all that night and was still raining the following morning, so we decided to abort the skiing and headed home. Ricky and Douglas dropped me off at my empty, disheveled apartment and continued their journey back to Long Island. I was alone, car-less, and depressed. The reality of my life was crystallizing and the picture was not very promising.

At age twenty-seven, I had everything that might fulfill one's life. But as cliché as it sounds, I really had nothing. I sat on my small balcony, beer in hand, and reflected on who I was, where I was, and where I was going. It was time to talk with God. We had dialogued many times and our conversations were as real to me as if I were talking to a friend at a coffeehouse. The moon was up, the rain had passed, and the stars were like flowers in full bloom on that relatively mild winter evening.

By three o'clock in the morning I was pretty well drained and had thanked God for the gifts of my life, my adventures, my friends, and my family. I had thanked Him for everything I had, and fully knew His majestic role in my existence. Then I moved on to question my future, its meaning, and my purpose in his grand design.

The conversation pivoted around the fact that I did not have a "best friend," a woman to share this life, and even though I had met some wonderful people along the way, I had always held back. I was never ready to commit, or perhaps had never found the right person, and had successfully avoided the bonds of a gold band on my left ring finger. However, at this point, I thought, maybe it was time to become a more productive member of the human race. Raising a family and propagating the species would be a worthy challenge and great goal for the rest of my life. It was time to graduate to the next phase of responsibility.

Somewhere around 3:30 a.m., I realized and clearly saw that if I had a significant other, my life would have much more meaning. From the recesses of my soul I sincerely thanked God for clarity in my life's direction and asked Him to put someone in my path who I could fall in love with: a big request and a good note with which to end the conversation. My eyes were heavy and I knew that my Monday morning patients were only four hours away. It was a short but restful sleep.

My first three patients were routine enough and I was able to retreat between patients to the sanctuary of my employer's office, where I would put my feet up on his desk, shut my eyes, and think about the previous night's conversation with God. It was the second car that I had totaled since I graduated dental school the year before. The first accident, three months prior (also with the casualty of a 280Z), did not have the impact on my life's vision as much as this one did. Sometimes you need the clang of a second alarm clock to wake you up. I knew that if something in my life did not change at this point, the next accident might not be as forgiving. I was not a bad driver, from my perspective, but for some reason, my cars kept getting mangled.

The hygienist entered the room at about ten o'clock and asked me if I would check her patient, without giving any indication that there was a very pretty girl waiting in her chair. Unmotivated, I took my feet from the desk and plodded towards the hygienist's room. As I entered the room and looked at the patient sitting there, I was awestruck. Yes, she was beautiful, with long brown hair, and a smile that beamed radiantly. Her high pronounced cheeckbones and bright green eyes jumped out at me. The hygienist introduced me and I shook hands with this new patient. It was her first appointment at the office, and she had been recommended to us by a friend. Four previous dentists had made her terrified of the dental experience and of the dental industry in general. She hid her fear well behind her pleasant smile. I examined her teeth professionally, told her that there was some work that needed to be done, and told the hygienist to schedule her for treatments. As I walked back towards my employer's private room, I looked up at the sky and smiled. This was not just another pretty face or someone with whom I could enjoy a meal or a movie. I felt a special connection in those few moments and believed that this was a setup divined by the ultimate matchmaker. "You work fast, don't you?" I said to God.

I would see this girl again for some dental treatment and knew that I would ask her out after the work was completed. Life seemed a little more focused for the next two months. I cleaned up my apartment, got another Datsun 280Z, straightened up my act, and looked forward to seeing the pretty girl from the hygiene room in my office on a weekly basis. Little did I realize that she was looking forward to her dental appointments as much as I was looking forward to seeing her.

On her final visit, two months later, I cemented a gold crown on the upper-right second molar. After the cement set, I stood in front of her and said, "If the bite feels funny, call me."

"Okay," she said.

"If it feels rough around the edges, call me."

"Okay," she said.

"If it is hot or cold sensitive, call me."

"Okay," she said

"May I ask you out socially?" I asked.

"Oh, oh, oh, ok," she stammered.

Surely it wasn't a fair way to ask her out. My psychology training was in full play with that tactless request for a date, but I got an "Oh, oh, oh, okay," and that was enough for me. Back in the office, my employer read me the riot act; he informed me that this patient was not just another girl to mark on my calendar. She was connected to one of the most well-known families in the community. Her brothers were six-foot six-inches and six-foot-four-inches tall, and her dad was a highly decorated Marine Raider not to be trifled with. If I was to date her, I had better be the quintessential gentleman, which for the most part I was. I respected women and cared for them the way my father cared for my mother. I wasn't worried about my behavior, but the two large brothers did give me some cause for concern.

I called her that same night. Her mother answered the phone. I found out later that Diana shook her head and waved her hands at my call, whispering, "I'm not here!" She did not want to take my call. Her mother bypassed Diana's protests and replied, "One moment, please. She is right here," and handed her daughter the phone. (Thank you very much Betty!) Diana informed me that her throat was a little sore and she did not know if she could go out that Friday night (March seventeenth, St. Patrick's Day 1978). I ended by saying, "I'll call you tomorrow and see how you're feeling."

I called on Tuesday, Wednesday, and again on Thursday. By Thursday she had broken down enough to say, "Well, okay, we can go out."

I picked her up Friday in my *new* light blue Datsun 280Z, and we went to a restaurant for dinner. Our date lasted until two in the morning and I knew that this was the real thing. The next morning I called my mom and asked her if she could define love for me and how one knows if he is in love. My mom replied, "Come on home, we need to talk".

Twenty-eight years later, entering the darkest moments of this cancer adventure, Diana's support and love helped to elevate me to a level where I could withstand the pain and torment of cancer's cure. She was by my side almost every waking (and sleeping) moment. At times when I couldn't move to reposition a blanket or even hold a cup so that I could take a sip of apple juice, she became my arms and fingertips. When I was blindly staring at the sky, she caressed my hair and whispered positive thoughts, or just sat beside me so that I wouldn't be alone. She even told me how pleasurable this time together was, which made me smile even more. From her viewpoint, we were sharing a moment of togetherness that our souls had not seen for some time. Life's business had occupied us, and this long span of time together was, in a bizarre way, special. We have had our ups and downs as most long-term couples do. We are from different communities, lifestyles, religions, and even different ends of the political spectrum, but our union was destined and I thank God for that.

Lessons

God answers our prayers; however, I believe there are some rules to asking and receiving what we request:

His time frame is not always in line with ours.

When we are really ready for a prayer to be answered, then and only then, is it appropriate to ask. Until then, we can accomplish most of our goals without divine intervention.

If a wish is granted, you need to recognize it and work with what is given to you. You will not be handed a pure, polished diamond. Often you will need to polish the edges and shine it up before you can see the full sparkle of the jewel before you. If you ask Diana, she would say that it took many years before she shined me up.

If a prayer has been answered, you must realize that the path from that point forward may not, and most likely will not, be exactly what you expect. Go with the flow and make it go right.

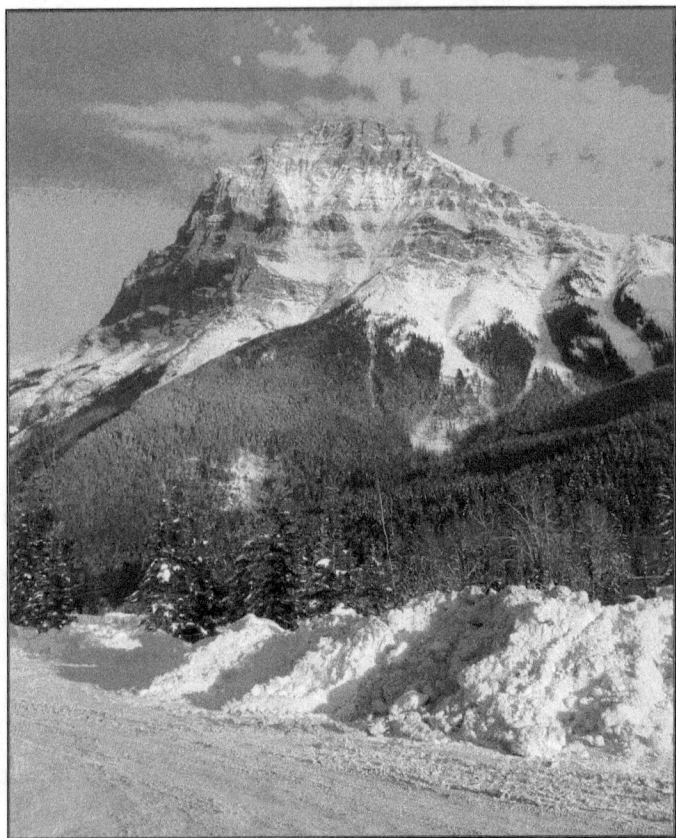

Mountain of Happiness

Life throws some curve balls at you and sometimes after your team hasn't scored a run in many innings, you can get quite frustrated. Nineteen eighty-nine was a rather lackluster year for my personal team. Actually, it was a rather lousy year. My brother had passed away; my dental practice had experienced major growth spurts which were creating a lot of stresses on me and my family; my son Michael was ill and needed surgery; my suction pump in the office (which is a main part and mandatory piece of dental equipment) had blown up, necessitating my closing the office for two days; and one Monday, my dental assistant did not show up and quit without giving notice.

As if a dentist without an assistant or a suction pump and with considerable stresses wasn't bad enough, the accounting system had been in error and somehow twenty-thousand dollars was not in an account where it should have been; in fact, it was nowhere to be found. Additionally the roof on my home was leaking, which was one of the reasons making it evident that we needed to take the financial plunge of gutting and remodeling the entire house.

It was time to talk to God. I walked downstairs, heading out to my backyard to have a discussion with the "Big Guy". My backyard overlooks a lake, and is as fine a place as any to converse with God. On my way out the door, a book that was on the coffee table caught my eye: I do not remember the book, and with exhaustive searching, still cannot find where the following quote comes from. I felt as if I was supposed to pick it up and read a verse or two before going outside. I do not know what compelled me to do so, but I followed the urge without hesitation.

Opening the book indiscriminately, I began to read.

"...as deep as your pit of despair is, that is as high as your mountain of happiness can be."

Well, that was an appropriate passage, I thought. Now I had a starting point for the conversation that was about to begin. I walked outside with that thought in mind, and began my talk, looking skyward with an angry attitude, I began my dialogue with God.

"Look, I'm about as low as I can possibly remember. Everything is going wrong. I'm not happy and if this is a big pit of despair that I am in, then I sure wish that You could throw a little more garbage on me. Go ahead and dump some more on me and make it a little worse. That way, my mountain of happiness can be that much higher when my life turns around. So, as long as I'm down this low, why don't You just keep heaping on more rubbish into my life?"

It was kind of bravado and bold and certainly an obnoxious way to begin a conversation with God, but I am sure that He has heard worse. After saying my piece, my short monologue was over. His response was no response at all. I could not hear anything. Even though I knew that He surrounded me, He was not responding to my tirade. Maybe I should not have been so harsh, but I was angry and I wanted Him to know the way I felt. With no response, I shrugged my shoulders and headed back towards the house, believing that the conversation was over. I had aired my views and now it was in His lap. He would probably answer me when I was in a less combative mood.

The rusty metal bottom of the rear sliding door was something else that needed to be replaced. As I entered the house, the raised edge caught the ball of my foot and ripped it almost completely off. That little pad just behind the big toe which is about a one inch circle on my size twelve foot, was completely peeled off except for one edge that just held on to the rest of my foot. The flap was about a quarter inch thick, cleanly separated from the rest of my body. I did not feel the pain right away, and the bleeding started slowly, but I knew that more pain and more blood were only moments away.

Hopping into the upstairs bathroom, I put my foot in the tub and turned on the cold water. Within moments, the pain in my foot was screaming and the water was crimson red.

My assessment of the situation: I would tape the flap in place and cover the wound with considerable bandaging on a daily basis and with considerable pressure, an elevated leg wrapped in ice, the bleeding should stop by the morning. Fortunately, I had had a tetanus shot within the previous two years, and the bleeding did stop.

Another thing to add to my list of problems and bad happenings, I thought as I wallowed with my leg propped on pillows. Then like a light bulb turning on in the blankness of my brain, I realized that God had responded to my verbal tantrum. Not only had He given me the appropriate passage to read before I talked to Him, He answered me by granting my wish of having my pit of despair dug deeper.

Every day for the next month, I was reminded of my discussion with the Big Guy because walking was painful, driving my car was painful, stepping on my dental rheostat was painful, and just sitting was painful. The healing took about four to six weeks and every day I was reminded to be careful what you ask for because you just might get it.

Fortunately, that was the bottom of my pit, and shortly there after the building of my mountain of happiness began.

Lessons

Unfortunately, in two thousand and five, the diagnosis of cancer met the mountain of happiness head on. It was a crossroad that reminded me of the conversation I had in my backyard with God sixteen years earlier. After the surgery, I looked at the cancer adventure as a very large divot taken from my mountain of happiness. However, I saw the love of so many family and friends that surrounds me, and I saw that this would strengthen my resolve to replace that divot and rebuild my mountain with more love and more happiness to an even higher level.

I have not taunted God at this point, asking to go any lower in any despair pit. I believe I have seen the bottom of the latest knock to my life and I beg Him and pleaded to Him that He grants my request of allowing my mountain to grow.

Life has ups and downs. Expect them and be thankful when you are up, and work hard when you are down to fill your valleys with love.

Before you converse with God, be sure you are not communicating in anger. You may be angry about your present circumstances, but don't dig a deeper hole for yourself by yelling at "The Man"

Wear shoes when walking outside at night.

Keep Breathing: Inspiration

I have taken each of my children on a world adventure of their choosing when they turned thirteen years or older. This adventure was a replacement for a Bar Mitzvah (the Jewish transition to adulthood), which was not conventionally celebrated in my home because I am Jewish and Diana is Catholic. My kids and I consider this "world adventure" the transition. Laurén chose to go skiing in Aspen Colorado; Michael chose to become scuba certified in the Cayman Islands; Bryan, our youngest, had analyzed the situation and one-upped his siblings with a ski trip to the European Alps.

So here we were in Courchevel, France, the best of the best, the most beautiful and largest ski area that Europe had to offer. Three feet of fresh powder on our first day of skiing promised to be nothing less than spectacular.

Diana had pleaded with me to hire a guide so that Bryan and I would not venture out of bounds and get into trouble. We are accomplished skiers and extremely capable of handling any terrain; after all, we are used to the ice, rocks, trees, crowds, and man-made snow of our New England ski slopes. Skiing on real snow would be easy, but to appease my wife, we hired a private guide who made the first part of our first day superb. We skied in powder up to our waists, steep and deep, and out of bounds where no one had tracked a mark. Our guide was outstanding and trained in detecting the avalanche areas, and she took us places that tested our skiing ability while taking our breath away with their scenic vistas.

After realizing that we were capable of handling anything, she asked if we would like to do some tree skiing. "Of course!" we immediately responded. Tree skiing affixes a little more adventure to the sport. The fact that there was so much snow allowed smaller trees to be hidden.

About halfway down the slope, my right ski had hit some hard immobile object that caught my leg and stopped my forward motion. My body twisted and threw off my balance plunging me into a head-first dive down the French mountainside. This in itself would have been dangerous, but the fact that there was three feet of fresh powder and I was negotiating a narrow passage between century-old pine trees created a scenario for disaster. Fortunately, I was wearing a helmet which initially saved my life as the top of my head smashed into the tree trunk.

The resultant collision directed my body downward into what is known as a tree well: the snow around the base of the tree that never really hardens. The warmth of the tree keeps the snow around it in a perpetual quicksand state. The powder that covers this warm snow disguises the tree well and if one happens upon it feet first, it is difficult to get out. Unfortunately, I went in head first, and bent at the waist.

Here I was, suspended upside down with my back firmly anchored against a tree, one ski off, and the other ski steadfastly embedded in three feet of powder. At this moment panic could have overtaken me. I was fifty-four years old, in moderate shape, fatigued by a half day of extreme skiing, and winded from this particular run. I had no leverage to escape, and every move sunk me even deeper into the tree well. I knew about tree wells from over forty-five years of previous skiing adventures. Other mountain guides had informed my friends and me of the dangers of tree wells, but I'd never expected to be upside down and backwards engulfed inside of one.

One's past experiences and education come into play at times like this. It turns out that the scuba training I had received fifteen years prior would help to save my life. Panic was not an option; understanding the danger I was in was paramount, and flailing arms and wrong motions would bury me deeper into the snow. My son and the guide were ahead of me on this particular run and would be of no value in helping me to recover. They were about fifty yards downhill, and even though my son had turned around and had started to climb uphill after hearing me crash, he would never make it before I suffocated.

At that moment there was only one crystal clear question to be answered: Is this how I was going to die?

"No!" I responded to my own question. As long as I had air I would have at least one minute to figure out how to get another inspiration.

I moved my head forward slightly and then backwards so that my helmeted head made a small pocket of air. With some difficulty I managed to get half a snow-filled breath. I did not move any other part of my body for fear of burying myself deeper in the snow. While I was doing that, I quickly assessed what position I might be in. I was bent at the waist, back to the tree, right ski off (I could feel my right foot wiggle), and left ski anchored in the snow, pointing downward. I had one chance to dislodge myself and hopefully get another breath of air on my way up. My limbs would be of minimal value, as they had no leverage against the powder.

The only place where I could attain leverage was from the tree, using my left ski as a counterbalance. After one more breath, I began my escape. My left hand curled between me and the tree and in one jerk, I slid my body to the right and pushed my left ski as firmly as I could into the snow. I simultaneously straightened my body as soon as it was dislodged from the tree. The bend in my midsection quickly straightened as well. While this was going on, I kicked my right leg and moved my right arm in a swimming motion. Most importantly, I snatched another gulp of air.

Unfortunately, this move only managed to untwist my body so I now lay face down, still buried under two feet of snow. Following a quick gulp of snow filled air, I kicked and clawed upward. As I finally surfaced, I twisted to face skyward and inhaled a substantial breath of heavenly air. I lay there exhausted but alive.

The frantic screams of my son echoed in my head. "Dad! Dad!" he yelled.

"I'm okay, Bry," I called with feeble vocal chords. "I'm okay. Stay where you are."

I was saved. As I said before, I was not supposed to die buried at the base of a tree well in Courchevel, France. Twenty minutes later I managed to completely uncover myself, find my right ski, and descend from my life-threatening fall.

Little did I realize that six months later I would be facing death again on the table of my surgeon. The cancer was probably with me at the time of my fall in France. Looking back, my decision to live and my ability to negotiate subsequent survival tactics appear miraculous. Now, three weeks after the surgery, I compare the two episodes. In France I had the ability to save my life from a natural disaster, and now I believe my survival from this potential medical disaster is still in my power. **I choose to live.** Once that decision is made, all I have to do is remind myself to take *another breath of air*. The surgery is complete and the chemotherapy will continue for nine more months. My self- motivation and the help of God will enable my survival.

Addendum
Respiration And Inspiration

I woke up one morning, weeks after my surgery, with two words battling each other at the tail end of my dream. They were **respiration** and **inspiration**. As a medically-trained individual, a lover of history, and a person who has full respect of the English language, I began to analyze the words that had been gifted to me during my slumber.

I broke each word down into its three component parts. Re-spir-ation: 'Ation' means 'the act of'; 'Re', means 'to do it again'; 'Spir', comes from Latin meaning 'to breathe' and also means 'spirit', relating to our souls.

The second word, "inspiration" has two main meanings, each of equal importance. I broke this word down with its component parts. "In" means "to enter or take in"; "spir" means 'breathe or spirit'; "ation" means "the act of." Using the first meaning, inspiration would mean to breathe as compared to respiration which would mean breathe in **again**, or continue to breathe. The physical life of our bodies is sustained by repeating this action. Another meaning of inspiration for many individuals is not simply defined by breaking the word into its component parts. Inspiration relates to a sensation of being touched by a divine connection, either seeing someone who inspires you, or makes you feel more powerful and strong. Or inspiration could be your own personal driving force that allows you to accomplish a difficult task. The divine component of this word inspiration combined with the **simple** inhalation of air, led me to believe that to be inspired all one needs do is 'breathe in air'.

"...**The Lord God formed the man from the dust of the ground and breathed into his nostrils the breath of life, and the man became a living being.**" (Genesis 2:7)

As the day went on, the word inspiration stayed firmly in my head with every breathe I took. I visualized being connected spiritually to everyone as they were breathing the same air as me. As long as I continued to inspire, I would continue to be connected and live.

Lessons

Every living creature relies on oxygen and its life-giving force. The air that we breathe has been recycled through many souls and it is what directly connects us to our past, present, and future. It's like a cosmic soup that we all share.

Keep breathing even if you are buried by three feet of snow.

Every breath you take can be inspirational to you and those around you.

There Are No Coincidences

On Tuesday, August 1, 2006, just one month short of the anniversary of my original cancer diagnosis, I doubled over in pain during my workday. Had the pain been anywhere but my stomach, I probably would have toughed it through and chalked it off to some routine bodily aches. Unfortunately, it was in my abdominal area, and my first thought was that I should at least call my oncologist.

My CT scan two months prior had shown no evidence of cancer recurrence. With that good news, my office staff had thrown me a surprise "survivor" party in June. The thought of cancer recurrence had not even entered our minds at this point, and life had settled back into its pre-cancer mode.

Carol, the physician's assistant (PA) of my oncologist, Jill, was pleasant and receptive to my call, and informed me that if I was concerned or if the pain did not dissipate shortly, then I should come in on the following morning. I cancelled my Tuesday afternoon patients and headed home to take some Pepto Bismal, lie down, and pray that this was just a stomachache.

Wednesday morning found me folded in pain, on the phone setting up an appointment to see my oncologist that morning. After an examination and some blood work, she sent me downstairs for an x-ray. It revealed a mass around my intestines but was diagnostically insufficient to pinpoint the problem. A few hours later in the hospital, I was drinking viscous, bitter white fluid preparing myself for a CT scan. The results of the scan would be ready on Thursday morning, and my surgeon, Dr. Salem, had made time to see me.

That Wednesday night, I was uncomfortable, but the pain began to lessen.

Early Thursday morning, Diana and I sat in Dr. Salem's office awaiting the previous evening's CT scan diagnosis. With his friendly face and solemn posture, flanked by his sweet assistant, Donna, and four or five medical students, Dr. Salem positioned himself to reveal the radiologist's report.

"I'm sorry to say, Robert, that the radiologist notes in his report that there appears to be a recurrent tumor surrounding the intestines causing blockage of the alimentary canal," Dr. Salem said. "It is very uncharacteristic for your type of cancer to recur this soon. It could be the Adenocarcinoma which could be very invasive, or it could be just in that one area."

He then went on to discuss the options and ideas regarding this twist in my medical condition. A procedure similar to the one performed a year ago seemed to be necessary (surgery and more chemotherapy); however, further investigation was suggested before he put me under the blade again.

"Is this something that needs to be handled immediately?" I asked.

"Well, I would like to check you into the hospital for some observation and more tests," he said.

"Well, I'm feeling better today and my stomach doesn't hurt as much as yesterday…."

"That could be caused by the barium drink that you had before the CT scan. It might have loosened your stool and allowed it to pass through the blockage."

"Well, if the blockage is unblocked at the moment and that invasive tumor does not invade too far, do you think I can go on vacation?"

"When are you supposed to go on vacation?"

"Tomorrow morning at six o'clock," I said.

"How long will you be gone for?"

"Two weeks," I answered.

His face grimaced a little, and then he responded.

"Where are you going?"

"I'm going to Ecuador, the Galapagos Islands, and the jungle to visit my daughter who left a year ago just after my surgery." His face went blank, and he hesitated before he spoke.

"I don't recommend it." he said.

The medical students and Donna also stared blankly at me. Here I sat with a potentially life-threatening blockage of my colon, and all I seemed to be concerned about was going on vacation.

During the two days of pain in my stomach, I had pondered my death. I knew that this vacation, this life experience, might be the last time that I spent with my children. I now had the choice of going into the hospital for observation or going to the Galapagos Islands and the rainforest with my kids. The choice was clear.

Against Dr. Salem's better judgment, I informed him that I would be gone for the next two weeks, shook his hand, and left the office. Diana agreed with me begrudgingly and knew in her heart that if this was to be my last vacation, then allowing me to go with her blessing might not be the smartest thing to do, but it would be the right thing to do for me. She had declined this trip six months prior when we booked it. A live-aboard boat to dive and tour the Galapagos and a several-day trek through the jungle was not her cup of tea. Michael, age 20, 17-year

-old Bryan, and I would go forward with our trip to visit my daughter at the end of her year of service.

At six in the morning the following day, the limo picked up the Rauch boys, and we began our journey to Ecuador. My stomach pains had calmed, but I was still aware that according to the radiologist the tumor had returned and my intestines were not right. Laurén had done some homework for me, as she was on the phone with us constantly from that Tuesday on. She found out that I could get back to the United States and home in under fifteen hours. A speedboat could be available to me in the Galapagos, and a charter plane from the main island could transport me to an airport where I could catch a plane home. Furthermore, she consulted the captain of our boat and the other areas where we would be staying in the jungle and along the way, about my diet. I would eat soups, fluids, and Jell-O, so as not to compound the existing blockage within my digestive tract. A close chiropractic friend, Jeff, even dropped off a protein shake mix and a vitamin compound for me on the eve of our departure. This would help my nutritional balance considering that I would be eating very little while adventuring.

While on the airplane to South America, I further considered the lunacy of my trip. Was I crazy? Had I lost my mind? This could turn out to be the worst decision I had ever made. Needless to say, I prayed to God every moment of the way, asking Him to grant me this time with my children without catastrophe.

The two-week vacation was spectacular, and I will gladly share our five hours of video with anyone who wants to sit and watch. At the end of our first week on a luxury catamaran in the Galapagos Islands, my guide asked me, "What was the favorite thing that you saw on the islands? Was it the birds, animals, terrain, fish?"

I responded before he finished his list: "It was watching my children hug each other, play with each other, and interact." The beauty of the Galapagos cannot be understated. It was magnificent. But from my perspective, as this might have been my last vacation, or last day, week or year on this planet, what ranked highest on my list of sights had no comparison.

We called Diana every day that we had cell phone service to inform her that my health had maintained status quo. We promised her that I would surely return home in one piece to face the medical issues with a broader smile and renewed faith and trust that God was on my side. He was helping me through and would help us through whatever lay ahead.

After leaving the Galapagos, we adventured throughout Ecuador and sojourned in the jungle for three days. The waterfalls, wildlife, foliage, and total package was breathtaking and revealed God's handiwork everywhere. Fortunately, my physical condition remained stable for this part of the journey also.

Two days after my return from Ecuador, I spoke with my oncologist and my surgeon. Both agreed that they should perform another CT scan, and it was scheduled for two weeks later. They also scheduled surgery for the week following my new CT scan, assuming that the results would show similar evidence of cancer recurrence.

They took the CT scan on Wednesday September 13th and I would not be seeing Dr. Salem to discuss the results until the following Monday: September 18th. Diana and I left the following day (Thursday) to spend my birthday weekend on Martha's Vineyard with some friends. Before leaving for the Vineyard, I needed to know that my other friends, who had been so supportive through the first cancer adventure, knew what was happening. Many of them already knew, having talked to and supported Diana during my Galapagos escapade. I wanted to touch base with them and hopefully see as many of them as I could before undergoing another grueling surgery. So, prior to leaving for Martha's Vineyard, I sent e-mails to friends in the vicinity of our home. I also made several calls to set up a "Surprise" Birthday Party for myself on the Monday evening after I was to see my physician and hear what the CT scan had shown. It would be a time for me to share with my loved ones the news that I would be in the hospital again, and that the support they shared the first time around would certainly be needed this time. My family and I would appreciate their love and prayers.

We went away for the weekend, and had a glorious time. I put behind me any thoughts of doom and gloom. There was no need to think about that; I would have enough time to ponder my situation after Monday's consultation. The weekend, like the trip to the Galapagos, was an exceptional jaunt with friends and my lovely Diana. We did not address the topic of my potential demise to any great length.

At Monday's appointment, Dr. Salem entered the room with a broad smile on his usually stoic face. Apparently, he explained, the new CT scan showed absolutely NO blockage, NO fluid, NO recurrence of the cancer, and NO need of a surgical procedure. He further explained that the first CT scan had displayed that my small intestine had rolled over upon itself giving the appearance of a tumor surrounding the intestine. This visual diagnosis was apparently an error in the reading of a two-dimensional film and a bigger error in labeling it as a tumor recurrence. Consequently, my trip to Ecuador, my fluid intake, my denial of my cancer recurrence, and time, had enabled me to unblock my balled-up small intestine.

Diana, Laurén, and I sat in disbelief, wanting to be euphoric, but not wanting to be overconfident that I was cured. We had been there before, and we were not ready for another disappointment.

I knew that those friends that I'd e-mailed for my surprise party were to meet us that evening at seven thirty for a night of drinks and pizza at Bertucci's. The "surprise" was for Diana. Though it was my birthday, my wife was the only one who didn't know about the party. And now, with our great news, our friends would get a great surprise as well. As it turned out, seventy-five friends came to my last-minute birthday celebration. Their excitement at our news elevated Diana's and my spirits to believe that this was truly the correct diagnosis and that the cancer had not and WOULD not reoccur.

The story does not end here. The feather in the cap, the clincher, the key incident of God's intervention had actually occurred that afternoon from my viewpoint. After I returned home from Dr. Salem's office, I was in my backyard contemplating the good news and envisioning what I would say to my friends that evening at my party. My cell phone rang and it was Al, my golfing partner, the guy who got that life-changing, God-inspired Hole in One. Al always called on the days of my doctors appointments, and I answered with a smile.

"Bob," he said, "I have good news for you. Your doctor is going to give you great news today!"

"I already saw the doctor," I told Al, "and it *was* good news. I don't have cancer. "

I paused a moment and then asked, "How did you know?"

He paused and then in his deep, unhurried voice explained,

"I got a hole in one today, Bob."

The silence on both ends of the line was deafening. He'd gotten a Hole in One, a second Hole in One on a second pivotal day of my life. Coincidence? I think not.

Lessons

There are no coincidences; only signs gifted to us that require our constant diligence to unravel the secrets that can help us enjoy our short time span on this planet.

Enjoy the journey today: every moment, every second, and every inspiring breath.

All we need to do is open our eyes and our hearts to see God's presence in our lives, and our journey will be fulfilled and rewarded with love.

Al and me

LOCAL GOLF

HOLE-IN-ONE
(At Twin Lakes CC)
Tim Ryan, using a pitching wedge, aced the 125-yard, 3rd hole. He was playing with Bill McInerney, Howie Mann and Marion Mann.

(At Orange Hills CC)
Al Bissonnette, using a 7-iron, scored a hole-in-one on the 148-yard, 3rd hole. He was playing with Bob Rauch.

(At Great River GC)
Bill Schaefer, using a 5-iron, aced the 127-yard sixth hole. He was playing with Randy Ball, Roger Baral and Frank Nuzzo.

WALLINGFORD CC
Member-Guest
Gross: John O'Connor-Chris Greider-Mike Greider-Bob Barker, 128. Net: Rich Lechetto-Donna

Al's first hole in one

Date	August 30, 2005

Name	Robert S. Rauch D.D.S.

Age	Fifty-five

Sex	Male

Diagnosis   Metastatic Mucinous Adenocarcenoma of the Appendix (Pseudomyxoma Peritonei), a rare form of cancer (1/250,000) with a 20% survival rate (internet statistic).

Treatment   1) Surgical intervention to remove the gelatinous composition of cancer cells that are dispersed through out the abdomen, along with removal of appendix, peritoneal lining, some spleen, and half of the colon: eleven hour surgical procedure.

2) Six sessions of belly bath chemotherapy where surgical tubing is inserted into the abdomen and Floxuridine (a chemotherapeutic agent) is administered for three days each session.

3) Twelve sessions of intravenous chemotherapy where Oxaliplatin, Leucovorin, Fluoroouracil, and Avastin were infiltrated into the circulatory system for three days each session.

4) Periodic CT scans to monitor any recurrence of the cancerous growth within the abdomen for the rest of this patient's life.

5) A firm belief that God exists and faith that He will guide and assist my survival through signs that I can follow.

My Personal Spiritual Signs & Notes

My Personal Spiritual Signs & Notes

For copies of this book
Contact LMB Publications
c/o: Dr. Robert S. Rauch
91 Cherry Street
Milford, CT 06460
203-874-5577
Or visit:
www.AlGotAHoleInOne.com

www.ingramcontent.com/pod-product-compliance
Lightning Source LLC
LaVergne TN
LVHW021401080426
835508LV00020B/2392